Thinking Skills and Early Childhood Education

Patrick J.M. Costello

David Fulton Publishers
London

David Fulton Publishers Ltd
Ormond House, 26–27 Boswell Street, London WC1N 3JD

First published in Great Britain by David Fulton Publishers 2000

Note: The right of Patrick Costello to be identified as the author of this work has been asserted by him in accordance with the Copyright, Designs and Patents Act 1988.

British Library Cataloguing in Publication Data
A catalogue record for this book is available from the British Library

ISBN 1–85346–551–8

Typeset by Elite Typesetting Techniques, Eastleigh, Hampshire
Printed in Great Britain by The Cromwell Press Ltd, Trowbridge, Wilts.

Contents

For Thomas Ronan

Acknowledgements

I would like to express my gratitude to the following, without whose support and collaboration it would not have been possible to write this book: John Adamson, Jan Ashford, Cynthia Beckett, Maggie Bowen, Judy Bralee, Ian Brown, Andy Cheatham, Charis Davies, Rachel Hewer, Jean Lewis, Jane Price, Pamela Rose, Joan Walker, Tracey Wiggan, and Jane Williams.

I am indebted to Richard Andrews and Sally Mitchell whose scholarship in the field of 'argument' is well known and with whom I have enjoyed working for many years. My thanks also go to the Esmée Fairbairn Charitable Trust for funding the research project which is outlined in Chapter 6. In particular, I wish to acknowledge the inspirational role of Matthew Lipman, who introduced me to the idea of developing children's philosophical thinking and whose work has brought about world-wide educational change.

Since I began undertaking research into the teaching and learning of thinking skills at St. Catherine's R.C. Junior and Infant School, Birmingham, in 1983, accounts of it have been published in a number of journals and books. As my central aim here is to present a unified conception of theory and practice in this field, with particular reference to early childhood education, I am grateful to the following for permission to draw on ideas and arguments presented previously, which have been extensively developed in this book: *Analytic Teaching*; the British Comparative and International Education Society; *Citizenship*; *Early Child Development and Care* (Gordon and Breach Science Publishers); Falmer Press; *If... Then: The Journal of Philosophical Enquiry in Education*; Independence Educational Publishers; Kluwer Academic Publishers; *Thinking: The Journal of Philosophy for Children*; University of North London Press; *Values Education*; *World Studies Journal*. For permission to quote from *Education for Citizenship and the Teaching of Democracy in Schools* and *From Thinking Skills to Thinking Classrooms*, I also thank the Qualifications and Curriculum Authority and Carol McGuinness respectively. As regards the latter publication, Crown copyright material is reproduced with the permission of the Controller of Her Majesty's Stationery Office.

The decision to use videotapes as a medium to enhance reasoning and argument in the early years of schooling came about as a result of my three-year-old son's enthusiasm for the *Sesame Street* television programmes. Therefore, I was particularly pleased when Charlotte Cole, Vice President (International Research) of Children's Television Workshop, permitted me to incorporate video clips from the series into my research in infant schools. She was also kind enough to provide additional materials to support the work being undertaken.

I offer this book as a contribution to the debate which is taking place at the present time about the nature and purpose of a 'thinking' curriculum. In so doing, I gratefully acknowledge the work of those teachers and pupils who participated in the projects which are discussed below. Finally, I am grateful to John Owens for his advice and support in the preparation of the volume.

Introduction

In recent years, a great deal of interest has been expressed, by teachers and researchers, in the idea that young children should be taught critical thinking skills as part of the formal school curriculum. In the USA and elsewhere, a number of programmes have been produced which aim to teach such skills (de Bono 1985, 1993; Paul *et al.* 1986, 1987; Lipman 1988, 1991, 1993; Harnadeck 1989; Cam 1995; Wilks 1995). While British research output on the teaching of critical thinking has not been as substantial as that in the USA, a number of major publications have appeared in the last ten years. The first two of these (Coles and Robinson 1989, Fisher 1990), present accounts of the major approaches to the subject and these have been followed by several texts which offer more individualistic approaches to practice (Fox 1996; Fisher, R. 1996, 1998; Quinn 1997). However, very little research has been reported on the teaching of critical thinking in early childhood education (the major exception here being the work of Murris (1992)). The central aims of this book are to offer a rationale for such teaching and to suggest ways in which it might take place in schools.

Accompanying a focus on critical thinking, there has also been a general concern at all levels within the educational system about students' ability to write essays, argue a case, debate, conduct small-group discussions and operate in other forms of spoken and written argument (Andrews 1995; Costello and Mitchell 1995b). Such anxiety is justifiable since teaching and learning the skills of argument are central to the educational enterprise. Indeed, one way of determining an individual's level of competence within a given discipline is to examine his/her ability to offer and to support arguments. Given this, I shall also suggest that such teaching should begin in the early years of a child's education.

Before examining the theory and practice of teaching thinking skills, with particular reference to early childhood education, I shall present an outline of the main themes of the book. In order to do this, it is necessary to make some introductory comments about my involvement in this field. I first became interested in the teaching of critical thinking in the early 1980s. At that time, my research focused principally on issues within the philosophy of education. In particular, I was concerned to examine the concept of 'indoctrination', to contrast it with terms such as 'education', 'training', 'schooling' etc. and to explore the extent to which indoctrinatory practices are evident in schools. As I progressed through the extensive literature on 'indoctrination', I became increasingly dissatisfied with analyses of the concept, offered by philosophers of education and others, who argued that it is necessarily a pejorative term, denoting, for example, unworthy intentions and teaching methodologies. In this, it was thought to be distinctive from 'education', which was viewed, by definition, as a 'good' thing, engaged in by well-meaning and enlightened individuals. As I shall suggest in Chapter 1, an adequate analysis of the concept of 'indoctrination' is rather more complex than much of the literature indicates. While it is certainly true that indoctrination is, at least in some sense, an illness which permeates educational institutions, it is also unavoidable (and therefore justifiable) in certain contexts. Furthermore, given the current prevalence of references to 'indoctrination' and 'indoctrinatory teaching' in the educational press and elsewhere, it is essential that student teachers and their more experienced colleagues should develop a sound understanding of this concept and consider the implications which this may have for their practice in schools.

Utilising the metaphor of an 'illness' to understand some of the forms and functions of indoctrination within educational settings was useful because it led me to seek a 'cure' or 'antidote' for them. Having made a distinction between justifiable and unjustifiable indoctrination and developed the view that certain indoctrinatory outcomes of the teaching process are to be combated, I looked for an appropriate educational vehicle to accomplish this task. In order to be successful, it seemed to me that any such approach would need to contain appropriate pedagogic materials which: (a) enabled children to learn the skills of thinking, reasoning and argument, and (b) were underpinned by a sound theoretical foundation. It was at this point that I became aware of Matthew Lipman's 'Philosophy for Children' programme through his *Thinking: The Journal of Philosophy for Children*. Coming from a background of philosophy myself, I immediately warmed to the idea that young children should be exposed to the teaching of logical, ethical (and more general philosophical) reasoning at a young age. Subsequently, I developed my own approach to the teaching of philosophy in primary schools, and undertook classroom-based research, the results of which were reported in my doctoral thesis (Costello 1990a).

As a result of co-directing a two-year research project, entitled 'Improving the Quality of Argument, 5–16' (together with a colleague at the University of Hull, Richard Andrews), I began to consider ways in which it would be possible to teach children the skills of argument in a broader, non-philosophical context. The project, which began in March, 1991, involved the participation of ten primary and ten secondary schools from Humberside and Lincolnshire. A final report was published which examines some of the theoretical issues underpinning the project and outlines and evaluates progress made in schools (Andrews *et al.* 1993).

In 1992, I participated in the Twelfth Annual International Conference on Critical Thinking and Educational Reform which was held at Sonoma State University in California. Attended by some 1250 delegates, the conference lays claim to being the largest forum for the discussion of critical thinking in the world. According to the conference proceedings, 289 presentations were made by contributors from Australia, Great Britain, Canada, Chile, Korea, South Africa, Switzerland and the USA. While many participants argued for the introduction of a 'thinking skills' curriculum into schools, it was only on seeing the vast number of books on the subject which were on sale at the conference that I came to understand the extent to which teaching thinking has become an integral part of educational provision in the USA and elsewhere.

Unfortunately, as I have noted above, this is not yet the case in Britain, despite the widely-held view that an essential aim of education is to promote effective thinking in children. One reason for such a state of affairs may be found in the rejoinder which is often made to those who advocate the introduction of a thinking skills component into the curricula of infant, primary and secondary schools, namely that: 'It is being done already'. Indeed, Robert Fisher (1990, p. vi) begins the introduction to his *Teaching Children to Think* by offering a quote from Gilbert Ryle: 'All lessons are lessons in thinking'. However, it is important to note that if this statement were to be regarded as true, books such as those mentioned above (and indeed this one) could not have been written. I wish to argue that the systematic teaching of thinking skills is an aspect of educational provision to which a great many children are not, at present, being exposed.

Two other reasons may help to account for the fact that relatively few books have been written on the subject of critical thinking in Britain. The first and most obvious is that teaching the skills of thinking, reasoning and argument is still a comparatively new enterprise in British schools. Since this is the case, we should not be surprised if texts outlining how such an educational goal might be achieved are comparatively few in number. However, the relative lack of emphasis on teaching thinking (and consequent paucity of published material in this area) is not due simply to the innovative nature of the enterprise. The educational and political context surrounding teachers who are attempting to introduce such work into their classrooms is also an important factor. The implementation of the National Curriculum, together with the elaborate mechanisms which were introduced for its assessment, have been responsible, to a considerable degree, for the emergence of the view that the essential task of education is to get children to focus on thinking about subjects, rather than thinking about their own thought processes (i.e. about thinking itself).

This narrowness of focus is, of course, replicated in teachers' reasoning about *their* practice. As a result of the recent reform of initial teacher education, such reflective enquiry is likely to become greatly restricted in scope. Indeed, the notion of school-based teacher training is itself the outcome of a philosophy which suggests that practice is 'better' than theory and that 'doing' is to be preferred to 'thinking'. That these categories are dependent on each other, rather than being mutually exclusive, is a precept which is at the heart of college- and university-based provision. The extent to which the developing partnership between schools and training institutions will encompass continued support for this principle remains to be seen. For my purposes here, I would only wish to suggest that a basic prerequisite of an educational system which seeks to encourage critical and creative thinking in children is that teachers themselves should be provided with opportunities to engage in these processes. Given this, it is hardly surprising that the development of a 'thinking skills' curriculum in British schools has taken place at a much slower rate than in their counterparts elsewhere in Europe and in the USA.

According to H. G. Wells, 'Human history becomes more and more a race between education and catastrophe'. The view that these two concepts are discrete entities, each competing to undermine and ultimately to eliminate the other, is often expressed. Yet despite the extended discourses and manifold insights, offered both by philosophers and philosophers of education, on the relationship between 'education' and 'catastrophe', the latter, in its various forms, appears to be as prominent as ever – on our television screens, in our newspapers, on our streets and, increasingly, in our schools.

In order to combat this, teachers are now being encouraged to place strong emphasis on the notion of 'moral values'. In its discussion paper, *Spiritual and Moral Development* (1995), the former School Curriculum and Assessment Authority (SCAA) suggested that 'Schools should be expected to uphold those values which contain moral absolutes' (p. 5). These include:

- telling the truth;
- keeping promises;
- respecting the rights and property of others;
- acting considerately towards others;
- helping those less fortunate and weaker than ourselves;
- taking personal responsibility for one's actions;
- self-discipline (p. 5).

In contrast, it was argued that bullying, cheating, deceit, cruelty, irresponsibility and dishonesty should be rejected. In offering this framework, SCAA outlined its views on the nature of moral development. 'Young children,' we were told, 'rarely have the ability or experience to make their own decisions as to what is right and wrong. Therefore they should grow up knowing which of these things are acceptable and which are not' (p. 5). However, as pupils grow older, they learn that moral values are the subject of discussion, debate and, indeed, controversy. In order to enable children to make up their own minds about issues such as divorce, abortion and blood sports, SCAA suggested that 'the task of schools, in partnership with the home, is to furnish pupils with the knowledge and the ability to question and reason which will enable them to develop their own value system and to make responsible decisions on such matters' (p. 6).

How is this to be achieved? My answer, in brief, is that the task should be approached on two fronts. Firstly, there is a need to teach children the skills of thinking, reasoning and argument. However, in order to become critical and reflective in their thinking, children require assistance from adults who themselves exhibit these qualities. The role of teacher education is of central importance here, since it should focus not simply on 'knowing, understanding and being able to do X', but also on *why* it is important to know X, understand Y, or be able to do Z. Within this perspective, it now becomes important for children and their teachers to discuss rather than simply to accept, to question rather than to acquiesce passively, to agree on the basis of shared understanding rather than because 'authority' will have it so. Of fundamental importance to this endeavour (and therefore basic to education itself) is the role of reasoned enquiry. Once this has been undermined in our institutions of learning, then whatever else is taking place therein, it is certainly not *education.*

The contents of the book are as follows. In Chapter 1, I offer a rationale for the teaching of thinking skills in early childhood education. I suggest that an essential aim of such education is to promote effective thinking in young children and examine a potential obstacle to achieving success in this undertaking: the problem of indoctrination in educational settings. The second chapter focuses on the nature and functions of 'education for citizenship' in the early years of schooling. In arguing that the teaching of thinking skills should be regarded as essential to any adequate notion of the term, I consider recent proposals to introduce citizenship into the curricula of schools and discuss in detail one aspect of it: education and cultural diversity.

In Chapter 3, I offer a response to the question 'Should young children be taught to think philosophically?' This is followed, in Chapter 4, by an examination of one important approach to teaching thinking skills, through the medium of philosophy. Annotated dialogues with young children are presented both here and in the appendices. In Chapters 5 and 6, teaching thinking skills through personal, social and moral education, and the teaching and learning of argument in early childhood education are examined. Once again, annotated dialogues are presented. Finally, in Chapter 7, I examine issues concerning the initial and in-service training of teachers for the early years, again with particular reference to developing children's thinking skills.

In order to write this book, it was necessary to read widely within the (now extensive) literature on early childhood education. In so doing, I was struck by the following comment which Kerry and Tollitt (1995, p. 1) make in the introduction to their book, *Teaching Infants*:

> The second distinctive feature of this book is that it makes frequent reference to research or to theoretical underpinning when considering and analysing practical teaching skills. There are precedents for this, of course, but rarely at the infant level of education... Most of the practical literature for teachers of this age-group is couched in the 'tips for teachers' format...

Although, as will be evident from the chapters which follow, much of the research which has been undertaken in the early years of schooling in recent years places strong emphasis on the examination of theoretical issues as a basis for the improvement of practice, nevertheless the above comment provides a useful yardstick against which educational publications may be judged. My concern here is to do justice to both the theory and the practice of teaching thinking skills in early childhood education. To this end, in regard to each of the topics discussed, I have provided a number of references to enable those readers who wish to do so to undertake further study in particular areas of interest. This is in keeping with one of the central arguments of the book, namely that in order to enhance children's thinking skills, teachers must themselves be willing to think critically about the aims and practice of education.

In summary, therefore, I am suggesting that teachers should:

- be provided with *opportunities* to think critically;
- receive explicit training in how to enhance *their own* critical thinking skills (as part of initial and in-service teacher education courses);
- receive explicit training in how to promote and extend *children's* thinking skills;
- demonstrate a *willingness* to think critically.

In writing this book, I would argue that the teaching of thinking skills has much to offer the curriculum of infant, primary and secondary schools. As regards the teaching and learning of individual subjects, the ability to discuss and to debate issues, to evaluate arguments, to question evidence, to formulate theories – in short, to think and to reason – is central to becoming a competent scientist, historian, mathematician etc. This work must begin in the infant classroom.

Chapter One

Thinking Skills and Early Childhood Education

My aim in this chapter is to offer a rationale for the teaching of thinking skills in early childhood education. I begin by discussing issues concerning: (1) the promotion of effective thinking in young children; (2) the contemporary context in which arguments for the teaching of thinking in schools are being proposed. As one major obstacle which is likely to impede pupils' intellectual development is the indoctrinatory nature of much of contemporary schooling, I examine several popular conceptions of 'indoctrination' and then argue for a new one. Having distinguished between justifiable and unjustifiable indoctrination, I offer a qualified justification for the use of the former in schools. I believe that it is necessary to adopt the perspective which I advance below in order to circumvent a difficulty encountered by many contributors to the 'indoctrination debate'. This arises as a result of regarding the concept simply as a term of abuse to describe the practices of others. By viewing 'indoctrination' in this way, one is rendered unable to differentiate between various kinds of teaching activities.

Promoting effective thinking in young children

An essential aim of early childhood education is to promote effective thinking in young children. To argue that 'Teachers should educate for thinking' is to make a statement which is somewhat akin to 'Education should be child-centred' or 'Teachers should encourage children to be creative': what is suggested seems to be manifestly worthwhile (Barrow and Woods 1988, p. 111). Many people make a more contentious claim. Not only is it desirable that children should be encouraged to think, they argue, it is also the case that schools are presently discharging their responsibilities in this area to the fullest possible extent. I would argue that this view is both complacent and misconceived.

Enabling children to speak, in a variety of situations and contexts, is of vital importance if we are to develop their thinking skills. Indeed, one of the central tenets of education is that children should be encouraged to talk about their work, their play, their interests, and so on (Fisher, J. 1996; Godwin and Perkins 1998). Yet the prejudice against speaking still holds sway in many quarters. The most common manifestation of this tendency is the fact that many parents tend to equate academic progress with 'what is in the books'. Since this is the case, teachers and student teachers often place an undue emphasis on activities which involve writing, in the belief that such work will provide the necessary evidence that something worthwhile has taken place in the classroom.

The idea that schools should engage in the systematic teaching of thinking skills is a relatively new one in British education. Whether this enterprise will be successful will depend, in part, on the importance which teachers and others accord to classroom discussion (Booth and Thornley-Hall 1991a, 1991b; Dillon 1994). Indeed, it is a curious anomaly that while speaking is regarded as an important aspect of early childhood education, its significance seems to decline as children get older, until, towards the end of their secondary education, pupils are once again imbued with the right (and the ability) to engage in discussion and debate. Over the past 16 years, my research has focused on the teaching of thinking skills (including philosophical thinking) to primary school children. As I shall argue in Chapter 3, philosophy (by which I mean a thorough endeavour to develop, clarify, justify and apply our thinking, principally, though not exclusively, with regard to the teaching of logical and ethical reasoning), provides an ideal means by which teachers may encourage children to articulate views, express arguments and reflect on their own thinking and that of others.

At first glance, the claim that children should be introduced to philosophy, as I have defined it, is a remarkable one. The sceptic might be forgiven, then, for reacting with incredulity to the argument which I wish to advance here, namely that children in the early years of their education are capable of engaging in philosophical discourse. However, several writers have argued convincingly that this is so. Perhaps the most well known book in this area is *Philosophy and the Young Child* by Gareth Matthews, in which he cites a number of instances of children displaying philosophical puzzlement. For example, Ursula (three years, four months) says: 'I have a pain in my tummy'. Her mother replies: 'You lie down and go to sleep and your pain will go away'. Ursula retorts: 'Where will it go?' (Matthews 1980, p. 17). According to Matthews: 'Ursula's question – "Where will it go?" – is an invitation to philosophical reflection. One can accept the invitation or not, as one chooses' (p. 18). All too often, adults are unwilling to engage children in such reflection.

A second example concerns the sort of thinking which may lead to philosophising at a later stage in the child's life. During a meal, Denis (three years, ten months) says:

> The bread's buttered already isn't it? So if we want it without butter we can't, can we? – unless we 'crape it off wiv a knife… and if we want it without butter and don't want to 'crape it off wiv a knife, we have to have it wiv butter, don't we? (p. 13).

Matthews argues that while:

> Denis is exploring the modal notions of possibility and necessity, which are central to the branch of logic called 'modal logic', this anecdote is perhaps pre-philosophical rather

than philosophical. It doesn't really pose a philosophical problem, let alone attempt to solve one. But it does incorporate the kind of play with concepts that nurtures philosophy (p. 14).

These examples illustrate the potential that young children have to engage in thinking about a range of issues.

Teaching thinking skills: the contemporary context

It would appear that the teaching of thinking skills in schools is an idea whose time has finally arrived. As I mentioned in the Introduction, while arguments for such teaching have been articulated and supported in the USA for many years, leading to a plethora of academic publications (Matthews 1984; Raths *et al.* 1986; Baron and Sternberg 1987; Ruggiero 1988; Healy 1990; Woditsch with Schmittroth 1991), progress in this field in the UK has been much more ponderous. Nowadays, however, those who have argued, over many years but with limited success, for the introduction of a thinking skills component into the curricula of schools, find both an educational and political climate that is encouraging of their efforts.

The question 'Why aren't thinking skills being taught?' was the subject of an article, written some years ago, by Matthew Lipman (1982) and has been asked by many authors since that time. One possible response to this question is that, for some years, philosophers of education and others have engaged in a wide-ranging debate about important theoretical issues in regard to which some clarity must be achieved before programmes for the development of children's thinking may be introduced into schools. For example, while some scholars have sought to clarify the concept of 'skill' (Barrow 1987; Smith 1987; Griffiths 1987), others have argued against this notion (Hart 1983). While some have asked the question 'are there general thinking skills?' (Schrag 1988; Andrews 1990), others have responded to it either negatively (McPeck 1981, 1990) or positively (Quinn 1994; Higgins and Baumfield 1998).

Although it is not my intention here to rehearse these differing perspectives, I do wish to argue for the existence of general thinking skills. This is for two reasons. Firstly, I agree with the views of Richard Paul (1993, p. 363), who, in a chapter subtitled 'Why critical thinking applies across disciplines and domains', suggests that: 'most significant and problematic issues require dialectical thought which crosses and goes beyond any one discipline… many interpretations and uses of discipline-specific information and procedures in exploring real-life issues are inevitably multi-logical'. Secondly, his critical thinking programme (Paul *et al.* 1986, 1987; Paul 1993) offers ample evidence to support the existence of general thinking skills, which may be taught and learned across subject disciplines. The argument model which I outline in Chapter 6 also deserves mention in this respect. As Paul *et al.* (1986, p. 9) argue:

A teacher committed to teaching for critical thinking must think beyond subject matter teaching to ends and objectives that transcend subject matter classification… She realises that... understanding a situation fully usually requires a synthesis of knowledge and insight from several subjects. She also sees that an in-depth understanding of one subject requires an understanding of others. One cannot answer questions in history, for example, without asking and answering related questions in psychology, sociology, etc.

This having been said, I would also agree with those who suggest that fostering children's thinking requires more than simply imparting a requisite list of skills and strategies: the cultivation of appropriate dispositions is also of vital importance. Authors disagree about the precise nature and extent of the dispositions to be encouraged in the classroom; however, Bonnett's concise list seems apposite: 'to be honest, responsible, open, and reflective' (1994, p. 111). In addition, Perkins (1993, p. 98) notes that 'Good thinking is more than skill and ability; it's a matter of commitment... To teach for thinking, it's not enough to teach skills and strategies. We need to create a culture that "enculturates" students into good thinking practices'.

During a keynote address to the annual North of England Education Conference, Carl Haywood referred to thinking as 'an educational imperative' (Haywood 1997, p. 26). He discussed an educational programme called *Bright Start*, which is designed for children aged between three and six years, and which:

> has the goals of stimulating the acquisition and elaboration of cognitive structures, of identifying and remediating deficient cognitive processes and of enhancing the development of... motivation, as well as of preparing children with the logic tools that they will need in order to succeed in the academic and social learning of the primary grades (p. 26).

Two important features of this programme are the distinctive teaching styles of those who teach it (referred to by Haywood as 'mediational teachers') and the resulting educational outcomes achieved by pupils. As regards the former, Haywood suggests that mediational teachers:

- ask questions;
- ask process-oriented questions;
- challenge responses, whether correct or incorrect;
- require justification of answers;
- promote transfer and generalisation of principles;
- emphasise order, structure and predictability;
- model the joy of learning for its own sake and as its own reward (p. 26).

According to Haywood, early studies have suggested that children who were exposed to *Bright Start* as part of their preschool experience:

> showed greater gains over six to eight months than did comparable children in IQ, in reasoning abilities, in language development, and in motor control (an aspect of self-

regulation), had a significantly greater probability of being placed in regular education classes, as opposed to special-education classes in the primary grades, *and to continue to avoid special-class placement* (p. 26).

Given outcomes such as the above, it is not surprising that the systematic teaching of thinking skills is now being regarded as an increasingly important element in raising standards of academic achievement (Barber 1999). In May, 1999, I was invited to attend a conference entitled 'From Thinking Schools to Thinking Classrooms'. The purpose of the conference was to launch a report, authored by Carol McGuinness and commissioned by the Department for Education and Employment, which outlines 'a review and evaluation of research into thinking skills and related areas' (McGuinness 1999, p. 1). The aims of the review were:

• to analyse what is currently understood by the term 'thinking skills' and their role in the learning process;
• to identify current approaches to developing children's thinking and to evaluate their effectiveness;
• to consider how teachers might be able to integrate thinking skills into their teaching – within subject areas and across the curriculum;
• to identify the role of information and communication technologies (ICT) in promoting a positive approach to thinking skills;
• to evaluate the general direction of current and future research and how it might translate into classroom practice (p. 3).

In a section of the report entitled 'Thinking Skills and Learning', McGuinness identifies several 'core concepts'. She argues that:

Although it may seem self-evident, focusing on thinking skills in the classroom is important because it *supports active cognitive processing which makes for better learning*. Thus, pupils are equipped to search out meaning and impose structure; to deal systematically, yet flexibly, with novel problems and situations; to adopt a critical attitude to information and argument, and to communicate effectively. Many writers argue that setting standards is not sufficient for raising standards. *Standards* can only be raised when attention is directed not only on what is to be learned but on *how children learn and how teachers intervene to achieve this...*

Developing thinking requires that interventions are made directly at the level of cognitive processing. If we want students to become better thinkers, we must make *explicit* what we mean by these better forms of thinking and devise ways *of educating directly for thinking* (p. 5).

In seeking to offer a rationale for the development of thinking skills, one further important issue must be addressed: the transfer of such skills across subject disciplines and, indeed, into aspects of children's lives outside school. Once again, this is a topic about which much has been written (Perkins and Salomon 1988, 1989; Bonnett 1995). Having identified three different kinds of cognitive intervention which might be used to enhance thinking skills (general approaches, subject specific approaches and an infusion methodology), McGuinness suggests that in each case 'maximising the transfer of learning beyond the context in which it was learned is at the heart of the matter' (p. 8). As we saw above, promoting transfer and generalisation of principles was a key aspect of the teaching style of the 'mediational' teachers referred to by Haywood.

There is now a substantial literature on early childhood education, including a number of general introductions to the subject (Robson and Smedley 1996; Bruce 1997; Smidt 1998). While authors in this field have focused on topics such as the National Curriculum (Anning 1995; Cox 1996), quality education (Abbott and Rodger 1994), effective education (Edwards and Knight 1994) and leadership in early childhood (Rodd 1998), comparatively little has been written on the teaching of thinking skills. This is true despite the frequent emphasis on children's cognitive processes. Some texts, however, are quite explicit about the importance of promoting thinking in the early years. For example, Whitebread (1996) cites both Lipman's Philosophy for Children programme (which I discuss in Chapter 3) and the work of Murris (1992). Athey (1990) focuses on children aged from two to five years and provides 'a detailed analysis and documentation of over 5000 observations collected by professionals, parents and students from 20 children during a two-year teaching programme' (p. xi). Nutbrown (1994, p. ix) writes about 'the promotion of high-quality thinking and action of children aged three to five years'. Celia and Sohan Modgil (1984) explore the development of thinking and reasoning in young children and Anning (1997, p. 26) discusses what she refers to as the 'cognitive curriculum'. As she explains:

> In the past teachers of young children have not emphasised cognitive development as high amongst their educational aims. In two studies of the aims of nursery teachers... [they] overwhelmingly emphasised 'social' aims. This contrasts with traditions of early years education in the USA where cognitive development is emphasised at the levels of curriculum planning, regular testing and economic accountability (p. 26).

Having suggested that there continues to be a great reluctance in Britain to support either the notion of a 'cognitive curriculum', or indeed the High/Scope curriculum which 'emphasises the need for each child to be directly involved in planning his or her own activities, negotiated with an adult, by a method known as "Plan-Do-Review"' (p. 27), Anning goes on to suggest that 'for many teachers of young children the new emphasis on teaching children how to think is exciting' (p. 27). However, before examining how such teaching might take place in schools, it is necessary to consider one potential obstacle to its success: the problem of indoctrination in educational settings.

Conceptions of 'indoctrination'

Some years ago, Ian Gregory (1973, p. 25) remarked that despite the 'highly embryonic state' in which the philosophy of education then found itself, one of the concepts which had received most attention from philosophers of education was 'indoctrination', about which, even at that time, much had been written. Three years earlier, Gregory and Woods (1970, p. 77) had noted the 'voluminous literature' devoted to 'indoctrination' and had expressed doubt that anything new could be said on the subject. Yet, 30 years later, we find that contributions on the topic (from both within and outside academic circles) are as numerous as ever; indeed discussions of indoctrination are, at the present time, very much in vogue.

I begin this section by making some introductory comments about the notion of 'indoctrination', which has been the subject of a number of songs, poems and novels. In 1980, the popular music group 'Pink Floyd' reached the top of the hit parade in Britain with a song which began as follows: 'We don't need no education. We don't need no thought control. No dark sarcasm in the classroom. Hey, teacher! Leave them kids alone!' According to Brenda Cohen (1982, p. 86), this song is an example of what she calls 'the extreme thesis in respect of education and indoctrination: the thesis that *everything* that goes on in the ordinary classrooms of apparently liberal societies is in fact indoctrination'. Furthermore, the song:

> suggests, as do more philosophical exponents of the position, that this indoctrination is carried on by subtle strategies – dark sarcasm for instance – rather than by overt means: so that while one curriculum is put forward and discussed by school boards and authorities, another, hidden curriculum is actually being more subtly projected (p. 86).

James Clavell's novel *The Children's Story*, presents a disturbing account of indoctrinatory teaching. In writing it, Clavell had in mind an educational experience undergone by his young daughter. He had been surprised to witness the vigour with which, on returning from school one day, she had chanted the Pledge of Allegiance to him, and had then claimed a dime in return. Clavell ascertained from his daughter that, according to her teacher, this was the appropriate payment which should be made by parents when the Pledge had been successfully recited.

He was disturbed to discover that, although her memorisation had been perfect, she was unable to tell him what certain key words such as 'pledge' and 'allegiance' meant. As Clavell (1982, p. 86) states: '*The Children's Story* came into being that day. It was then that I realized how completely vulnerable my child's mind was – any mind for that matter – under controlled circumstances.' This novel, dealing with the indoctrination of a group of children which took place in exactly twenty-five minutes, gave the author much satisfaction because it forced him persistently to ask certain questions, such as: 'what's the use of "I pledge allegiance" without understanding? Like why is it so easy to direct thoughts and implant others? Like what is freedom and why is it so hard to explain ?' (p. 87).

These questions evoke a popular conception of the term 'indoctrination' which sees its application solely in the context of the political situation in Eastern Europe prior to the demise of Communism in the former USSR. During the present decade, a number of countries have been subject to dramatic internal change and, as a result, several graphic accounts of the indoctrinatory practices utilised within their educational systems have come to prominence (Louis 1990; Rich 1990; Spencer 1990; Sharma 1996; Leigh 1997). I want to argue that these accounts, while symptomatic of what many people believe to be the essence of indoctrinatory teaching, are, in reality, only partly constitutive of it. In short, I shall suggest that the spectre of indoctrination is all too evident within the educational systems of countries with long-established democracies.

To see that this is so, one has only to read books like *Lies My Teacher Told Me* (Loewen 1996), a national best-seller in the USA and aptly subtitled: *Everything Your American History Textbook Got Wrong*. Over the past 15 years in the UK, headlines such as the following have frequently appeared in national newspapers or *The Times Educational Supplement*: 'Should adults be allowed to indoctrinate children in any way they choose?' (Humphrey 1997); 'O come all ye faithful?' (Adler and Mason 1998); 'Thatcher has her way over school history' (Judd 1990); 'Why state education is bad for children' (Scruton 1990); 'Call to outlaw preaching of politics in schools' (Passmore 1985); 'Tories declare war on indoctrination' (*The Times Educational Supplement*, 7 March 1986, p. 6), 'Warning on propaganda posing as peace studies' (*The Times Educational Supplement*, 27 July 1983, p. 8); 'World Studies "propaganda" – Scruton' (*The Times Educational Supplement*, 13 December 1985, p. 5) etc.

This latter article refers to a pamphlet by Roger Scruton (1985) in which he argues that World Studies teaching is indoctrinatory rather than educational. A second pamphlet, of which Scruton is co-author, makes a similar attack on Peace Studies, and takes a passing swipe at 'Women's Studies', 'Black Studies', 'Gay Studies' and 'Sports Studies' (Cox and Scruton 1984). A third pamphlet, again co-written by Scruton, offers a Draft Amendment to the 1944 Education Act, which recommends stern action to be taken against those teachers who seek to indoctrinate their pupils (Scruton *et al.*, 1985).

We must now ask whether the numerous accounts of 'indoctrination' which have been offered over the years by philosophers of education have contributed anything to the above discussions. A charitable answer to this question is 'very little'. Indeed, it seems to me that many suggested conceptions have succeeded only in blurring vital distinctions, an appreciation of which would lead to a long overdue reappraisal of the term.

Gatchel (1972) has argued that viewing 'indoctrination' with opprobrium is a comparatively recent development in the world of education. Historically the term simply meant 'teaching doctrines', and was not looked upon as what philosophers call a 'boo' word , i.e. something to be given a negative value. Nowadays, however, 'indoctrination' is seen as a term to be compared unfavourably with, for example, 'education', which is seen as having positive value in itself. Thus, while 'indoctrinating' is thought to be the concern of Communists (Garforth 1962), Roman Catholics (Hare 1964; Flew 1972a, 1972b), pacifists (Sale 1984), and certain other proponents of political education (Scruton *et al.*, 1985), 'educating' is said to be what we 'good' teachers are engaged in.

This myopic view of indoctrination is safeguarded, to some extent, by the arguments of philosophers who assert that 'indoctrination' is a matter of the methods used by the teacher, or the subject matter conveyed to students, or the teacher's intention to indoctrinate. Various combinations of these features have also been suggested as providing the 'essence' of the term. A fourth alternative, which views 'indoctrination' in terms of the outcome or result of a teaching transaction, has been ignored by many authors, and where it is mentioned, it is often either: (1) treated briefly and summarily rejected, or (2) linked (mistakenly, in my view) to other criteria, for example 'non-evidential, non-critical belief' (Siegel 1991, p. 31). I shall argue that this notion of *result* is central to the concept.

In a number of educational writings, a disturbing trend has become evident. The term 'indoctrination' is used to refer to the inculcation of those values with which the writer disagrees, while 'education' is said to involve inducting into values of which he/she approves. A good example of this tendency can be found in *Education and Indoctrination*, in which the authors (Scruton *et al.*, 1985, pp. 25–26) suggest that there are five elements which constitute 'indoctrination':

(1) Conclusions are foregone…
(2) The conclusions form part of a constellation, whose meaning is to be found in a 'hidden unity', based [on an] emotional or political attitude.
(3) The conclusions are premises to action, and form the fundamental starting-point of a political 'programme'.
(4) The conclusions are part of a closed system of mutually confirming dogma, which serves to consolidate and validate the emotional unity from which it springs.
(5) They are typically established not by open discussion, but by closing the mind to alternative viewpoints, and perhaps even by vilifying or denouncing opposition.

An examination of this pamphlet reveals that the term 'indoctrination' has been used to denote those values which Scruton *et al.* do not wish to see introduced into educational institutions. However, it is significant that religious education, which has traditionally been viewed as a paradigm case of indoctrination (Flew 1972a, 1972b; Kazepides 1991; see also Leahy and Laura 1997), is not included for censure. Indeed we are told that religion forms 'an ineliminable part of our constitution as rational beings' (Scruton *et al.* 1985, p. 45). Given that substantial arguments have been advanced against such a view, one thing becomes clear from this brief explication. We need to do more than to use the term 'indoctrination' simply to indicate those values which we do not share, if it is to function meaningfully within the realm of educational discourse. We must have a criterion which we are able to apply without fear or favour to *all* values. In what follows, I shall attempt to provide such a criterion.

In looking for a plausible characteristic (or set of characteristics) in terms of which 'indoctrination' might be defined, philosophers of education have sought a set of necessary and sufficient conditions for applying the concept. Those who have posited a particular content as being central to the term, have pinned their arguments on a supposed conceptual link between 'indoctrination' and 'doctrines' (Spiecker 1987, 1991; Kazepides 1991). This approach has been summed up in Antony Flew's bold statement, 'No doctrines, no indoctrination!' (1972b, p. 114). However, Flew's claim cannot be sustained, since it has been argued convincingly that it is possible to indoctrinate not only doctrines but also true and false propositions (Thiessen 1982). In short, content of a doctrinal nature is not a necessary condition of 'indoctrination'.

Let us now turn our attention to another criterion which, it is argued, is constitutive of 'indoctrination', namely intention. A number of philosophers have given support to the view that for indoctrination to be taking place, for example in a classroom, the teacher must *intend* to indoctrinate (White 1972; Snook 1972a, 1972b; Beehler 1985; Spiecker 1991). On this argument, unintentional indoctrination is ruled out by definition. To rebut such an inference, we may invoke a well-worn but effective epigram: 'The road to indoctrination is paved with good (as well as bad) intentions'. This, I believe, precisely locates the major weakness in arguments supporting the intention thesis, since it is possible for teachers to indoctrinate their pupils *unintentionally*.

For example, Cooper (1973) argues that unintentional indoctrination may be engaged in by indoctrinators whom he terms 'sincere'. A 'sincere' indoctrinator is defined as 'one who himself believes the propositions he is teaching, and who thinks it important that his students should believe them precisely because, according to him they are true' (p. 44). While it should be noted that it is not only 'sincere' indoctrinators (as defined by Cooper) who can unintentionally indoctrinate, the existence of such a group poses a problem for Ivan Snook, a leading proponent of the 'intention' criterion. Snook (1972a, p. 50) argues, on the one hand, for a 'strong' sense of 'intention', so that someone is indoctrinating if 'in his teaching he is actively desiring that the pupils believe what he is teaching regardless of the evidence'. However, this can be criticised because sincere indoctrinators, believing the propositions they teach to be true, and not being aware of any evidence which they would consider as sufficient to count against them, therefore cannot intend for their students to believe such propositions 'regardless of the evidence'. Indeed, they might well state that, were satisfactory evidence to be provided against a proposition p, then they would not wish their students to believe that p is true (Cooper 1973).

Snook (1972a, p. 50) also offers a 'weak' sense of 'intention' so that a person is indoctrinating if he/she foresees it as 'likely or inevitable' that, as a result of his/her teaching, pupils will believe what is being taught regardless of the evidence. This attempt to expand the meaning of 'intention' has also been shown to be unsatisfactory, and its demise brings with it the collapse of the 'intention' criterion (Kleinig 1982). Since convincing arguments can be adduced to support the view that one can indoctrinate unintentionally, we must conclude that attempts to establish 'intention' as a necessary condition of 'indoctrination' have been unsuccessful.

Several writers have argued that 'method' is essential to an understanding of 'indoctrination' (Moore 1972; Barrow 1975; O'Hear 1995). On this view, whether a teacher is engaged in indoctrinating his/her pupils depends on *how* he/she teaches them. Thomas Benson (1975) has argued that there are two main forms of indoctrinatory method: the persuasive presentation and the engineering of assent. Each form has two sub-categories. The biased argument and the dogmatic presentation are illustrative of the persuasive presentation, while deprivation of the ability and of the opportunity to withhold assent from a proposition, belong to the engineering of assent.

We must now ask: (1) Is 'method' a necessary condition of 'indoctrination'? (2) Is 'method' a sufficient condition of 'indoctrination'? In one sense, the answer to the first question is 'no' since, as I shall argue presently, a child may become indoctrinated by *rational* methods. Indoctrinatory (i.e. non-rational) methods are, however, both necessary and justifiable in early childhood education (Wagner 1978). Now if my analysis of 'indoctrination' is acceptable, it will become clear that such methods are not a *sufficient* condition of 'indoctrination'. To see that this is so, we need do no more than to imagine a young child with whom we have employed indoctrinatory methods, but who remains uninfluenced by them, and who therefore does not end up in an indoctrinated state of mind.

The idea that it is necessary to use indoctrinatory methods with young children is one which many writers are unwilling (or unable) to accept. However, the arguments which they offer against this thesis are unconvincing. The tactic usually adopted is to suggest that no part of early childhood education can be called indoctrination if the teacher *intends* that the child will be able to reflect critically, at a later time, on the beliefs into which he/she has been inducted (Thompson 1972; see also McLaughlin 1984; Siegel 1991). 'Intention' has already been shown to be inadequate as a criterion of 'indoctrination'. Brenda Cohen (1981, p. 51) is correct when she asserts that 'if Snook is right and these methods are in fact necessary where very young children are concerned... then it may be preferable to concede that there is an area where indoctrination is acceptable.'

Is indoctrination ever justifiable?

In examining a fourth criterion of 'indoctrination', I propose to concentrate on two articles by Paul O'Leary. He is concerned to remedy a deficiency in previously written work on 'indoctrination', namely a tendency to concentrate on analysing statements such as 'X is indoctrinating Y' rather than 'Y is indoctrinated'. He offers two descriptions of the indoctrinated state of mind, both of which, I shall argue, while contributing something to an adequate understanding of 'indoctrination', are ultimately unsatisfactory.

O'Leary (1979, p. 295) begins his first article by suggesting that according to Ivan Snook:

> there appear to be three general conditions which conjointly are necessary and sufficient to claim that someone is indoctrinated. These are: (1) the belief condition – the indoctrinated person believes a proposition or set of propositions; (2) the epistemic condition – the indoctrinated person believes a proposition or set of propositions 'regardless of the evidence'; (3) the causal condition – the belief condition and the epistemic condition have been brought about because of certain teaching activities.

O'Leary reformulates the belief condition to include the notion of 'doubting that p', and includes a dispositional condition, so that his first description of the indoctrinated state of mind is as follows: 'S believes that p or doubts that p regardless of the evidence and is disposed to reject any q which is offered as a counter-instance to believing that p or doubting that p' (p. 299). By 1982, O'Leary's definition had undergone certain important changes. His second formulation is: 'Because of T's teaching, S believes that p, regardless of the evidence; and is disposed to reject any q that is offered as a counter-instance to believing that p' (1982, p. 77).

The following points should be noted: (1) the notion of 'doubting that p' has been left out in the second definition; (2) O' Leary offers a causal condition which is absent in his earlier article. As far as the belief condition is concerned, I can see no reason to reject O'Leary's earlier view that belief and doubt are disjunctively necessary for an adequate understanding of the indoctrinated state of mind. O'Leary himself offers us no reasons as to why he has decided to dispense with the notion of 'doubting that p' . It would seem that just as teachers may teach for unquestionable belief, so too may they teach for unquestionable doubt. On the traditional view of indoctrination, they can only be accused of indoctrinating if they wish their pupils to *believe* something unshakably. This would surely allow teachers who are concerned only to *discredit* certain views, while perhaps offering nothing in their place, to escape the charge of unjustifiable indoctrination. They teach for unquestionable doubt, not for unquestionable belief. So widening the belief condition to include the notion of 'doubting that p' will allow us to bring what such teachers do within the purview of indoctrination, and so within the realm of culpability.

Turning to the epistemic condition, O'Leary argues that the phrase 'regardless of the evidence' can be interpreted in two ways, since a person can believe or doubt a proposition *without* evidence, or *despite* the evidence. Now while it is no doubt the case that indoctrinated people often believe propositions without or despite the evidence, this is surely not a *necessary* condition of their being in an indoctrinated state of mind. If I teach children to believe that 'two plus two equals four' in such a way that they reject all counter-instances to believing it, does this necessarily imply that they believe it *without* evidence? Certainly it may be the case that these children have come to believe it as a result of learning it by rote, and so have no evidence for it. But, equally plausibly, they may have come to believe it as a result of a practical demonstration using four cubes. Similarly with a whole host of propositions from all academic subjects. Children may be indoctrinated with regard to a proposition although they have come to believe it not without evidence, or despite the evidence, but simply *because of* the evidence.

As we have seen, O'Leary's causal condition features only in his second formulation of the indoctrinated state of mind. The inclusion of such a condition is considered necessary in order to distinguish between a person who holds a view in a fixed way because of someone's teaching, and a person who exhibits a similar tendency due to having been in a motor accident (Snook 1972a, p. 40) or because of stupidity or an unwillingness to think for himself/herself (Degenhardt 1976, p. 26). Yet even if we agree with Degenhardt (p. 26) that 'indoctrination does have to be the result of human agency or action', it still seems to be the case that O'Leary's causal condition ('Because of T's teaching') is too limiting.

To begin with, it is not always the case that a charge of indoctrination can be levelled at a *particular* teacher. As Nancy Glock (1975, p. ii) suggests: '"indoctrination" need not apply only to the… actions of individuals. It can refer… to such policies and practices of *institutions* as do tend to produce indoctrinatory outcomes.' If the central aim of a certain school is to produce religious conviction in its pupils, it may be impossible to attribute a child's indoctrinated state of mind to an individual teacher. Rather, it is more likely that the school's ethos is responsible for producing a child who responds in a certain way to the inculcation of religious beliefs. Mr Smith or Ms Jones may do very little as individuals to promote such beliefs, and yet children may become indoctrinated as a result of a particular lesson, or series of lessons, given by them. Such indoctrination may have very little to do with the lessons themselves – it is possible that teaching received from previous teachers, or at school assemblies, etc., may have contributed substantially to the formation of fixed religious beliefs.

Similarly, a substantial number of other influences may be exerted on the child, for example, by parents and friends, newspapers, television and the Internet, and these may combine to produce someone who is 'ripe' for indoctrination. It may therefore be unjust (as well as misleading) to accuse a particular teacher of unjustifiable indoctrination, simply because some of the children in his/her class end up in an indoctrinated state of mind as a result of a particular lesson. As William Hare (1979, p. 66) notes:

> We cannot, of course, *infer* from the fact that pupils emerge from school with closed minds that their teachers failed to teach in an open-minded way. There may be many forces at work in the homes of students, and in society at large, which make the open-minded attitudes of teachers ineffective.

However, this is not to suggest that outside influences on the child always serve to exculpate a teacher accused of unjustifiably indoctrinating his/her class. Such a teacher cannot refute the charge simply by reminding us that children are subject to such influences, and by maintaining that it is these influences, and not his/her teaching, which have led to their developing an indoctrinated state of mind. To determine whether or not the teacher in question has indoctrinated his/her pupils unjustifiably, we need: (1) to determine whether such pupils are in fact indoctrinated and (2) to examine his/her conduct during the lesson(s) in question. It is at this point that content, method and intention are likely to provide us with vital clues in our enquiry. We need to ask whether the teacher's input into the lesson(s) is of the sort which tends to lead to indoctrinatory outcomes (Glock 1975; Beehler 1985). We also need to examine the ethos of the school itself, and such external factors as have already been mentioned. Everything will depend on the particular circumstances of the case. It is on the basis of these considerations, taken together, that we can make a judgement about the teacher's culpability.

To ascertain whether or not indoctrination has taken place during a particular lesson or series of lessons and, if so, what (if anything) it is about those lessons which was indoctrinatory, is by no means easy, and it is not my intention here to examine the issue in any depth. Rather, I am concerned to argue that to attribute a child's indoctrinated state of mind to a particular teacher as O'Leary does, is not always justifiable. Therefore, I propose to adopt a modified causal condition, which is: 'due to the teaching or influence of Y'. This has the advantage of attributing indoctrination to factors outside a particular classroom, and therefore outside the control of a particular teacher. 'Y' will include institutions, teachers, parents, friends, the media, etc.

O'Leary's first formulation of the dispositional condition is as follows: 'S... is disposed to reject any q which is offered as a counter-instance to believing that p or doubting that p'. Now 'q' is ambiguous here, since it is open to two interpretations: (1) a counter-instance which appeals to a present state of affairs or knowledge (for example, 'Paris is the capital of France not of Italy'); (2) a counter-instance which appeals to a putative future state of affairs or knowledge (for example, a possible response to someone who maintains that a Conservative government would improve the state of the National Health Service might be: 'But what if a Conservative government actually closed down more hospitals than its predecessors?').

Further implications now ensue, since we must ask whether the term 'indoctrinated' can be said to apply to either or both of the following: (1) persons who reject counter-instances to their believing that p or doubting that p at the time at which they are offered to them, but who later accept such counter-instances; (2) persons who reject such counter-instances at the time at which they are offered to them, and at all times in the future. White (1972) maintains that only a person who falls into the latter category can be called 'indoctrinated', since his/her beliefs are 'unshakable'. However, I wish to argue (along with Callan (1985)) that we can call someone 'indoctrinated' even though this state of mind may only be a temporary one. Furthermore, for us to be able to refer to someone as 'indoctrinated', it is only necessary that he/she rejects any *present* counter-instance at the time at which it is offered to him/her. It is not necessary that such an individual rejects any putative future counter-instance. For example, let us say that I attempt to indoctrinate a child with a proposition such as 'There are ten rings around the planet Uranus'. In order for me to be able to say that I have succeeded (i.e. that the child has become indoctrinated), it is necessary only that the child rejects present counter-instances to the proposition (for example, 'Uranus has nine rings around it'). It is not incumbent upon him/her to reject a putative future counter-instance (for example, 'What if an eleventh ring were to be discovered in 2001?'). This is an important distinction of which O'Leary's analysis fails to take account. Accordingly, 'any q' in his schema must be amended to 'any present q'.

My definition of the 'achievement' aspect of 'indoctrination' can now be stated thus:

> X is indoctrinated with respect to p (a proposition or set of propositions) if, due to the teaching or influence of Y, X believes that p or doubts that p, in such a way that X is disposed to reject any present q which is offered as a counter-instance to believing that p or doubting that p.

Looked at from the point of view of the indoctrinator, the formula becomes:

> Y indoctrinates X with respect to p (a proposition or set of propositions) if Y teaches or influences X to believe that p or doubt that p, in such a way that X is disposed to reject any present q which is offered as a counter-instance to believing that p or doubting that p.

This formulation also implies the achievement of an indoctrinated state of mind. Rather than to suggest that a teacher who failed to bring about such a state of mind in his/her pupils was engaged in indoctrinating them, it is preferable to say instead that he/she was *attempting* to indoctrinate them (Kleinig 1982, p. 59). Or, in cases where we suppose that no intention to indoctrinate is involved on the part of the teacher, we might say that the teaching or influencing of his/her pupils was such that it *tended towards* an indoctrinatory outcome (compare with Beehler 1985, p. 266). In discussing whether or not being in an indoctrinated state of mind is desirable, O'Leary borrows a phrase from Gilbert Ryle (1949, p. 141) and suggests that when a person is in such a state he/she is not 'prepared for *variable* calls within certain ranges'. He continues:

> Whether being in a state of mind appropriate to indoctrination is educationally harmful, depends upon (1) whether knowing how to engage in a given activity is thought to be important and (2) whether we construe the activity that students are being taught as subject to variation... suppose that knowing how to engage in a given activity is regarded as important, but that the beliefs, skills, and dispositions required for its performance are perfectly suited to all circumstances and not subject to alteration. If we knew that a given activity would require no modifications in belief in order to perform it with a minimum degree of competence, then there would be no educational objection to bringing about that state of mind that is characteristic of being indoctrinated (1982, p. 80).

O'Leary's discussion concentrates on the teaching of *activities* to students. While engaging in such activities necessarily involves the acquisition of certain beliefs, skills and dispositions, I see no reason why Ryle's passage cannot be used to refer to the teaching of beliefs seen as ends in themselves. Thus it becomes possible to say that when a given belief is not subject to '*variable* calls within certain ranges' (i.e. when there exists, to the best of our knowledge, no warrantable alternative to it), it is justifiable to indoctrinate a child with that belief. The following is a representative sample of beliefs with which children, on this criterion, may justifiably be indoctrinated:

> Two plus two equals four.
> Darkness is the absence of light.
> Human beings need food and water to stay alive.
> King Henry VIII had six wives.
> Rome is the capital of Italy.
> In French, 'lundi' means 'Monday'.
> The chemical symbol for copper is Cu.
> The poem 'Days' was written by Philip Larkin.
> The green pigment contained in the leaves of plants is called chlorophyll.
> The balance of visible trade is said to be in surplus if exports exceed imports.
> *Les Demoiselles d'Avignon* was Picasso's first Cubist painting.
> All triangles have three sides.
> A minim is a musical note that equals two crotchets in time value.
> Trotskyism is a form of Communism supporting the views of Leon Trotsky.
> The Koran is the sacred book of Islam.
> The Lateran Treaty of 1929 established the Vatican City as an independent sovereign state.
> Ohm's Law is expressed in the equation: electromotive force (in volts) = current (in amperes) x resistance (in ohms).

Some comments must be made about the above list. To begin with, it will be noted that the propositions offered cover a wide range of topics. Indeed it is possible to indoctrinate beliefs (as expressed by propositions) in all school subjects, at all levels within the educational system. Secondly, the beliefs to be indoctrinated are all *true* beliefs (i.e. they represent knowledge in various fields). Consequently, such counter-instances as may be offered (expressed as propositions) will be *false*. Thirdly, therefore, these (what I shall call category 'A') beliefs do not admit justifiable alternatives (for example, one would not be warranted in maintaining that some triangles do not have three sides, or that acid will turn red litmus paper blue 'one day'). Category 'A' beliefs represent the state of knowledge as it is (or as we believe it to be) at the time we are engaged in indoctrinating them.

Let us now contrast the above propositions with a list of statements which express value judgements. For example:

Art is imaginative expression.

One should never steal under any circumstances.

The Conservative Party offers the most credible alternative to a Labour government.

The Pope is infallible when he speaks *ex cathedra* to define a doctrine concerning faith or morals.

How are these two categories of statement to be distinguished? To begin with, one should say that as regards the latter set of beliefs (which I shall include in category 'B'),[1] it is possible for two people who are equally well-informed about the nature of economics, aesthetics, morals, politics and religion, to disagree about them without either party necessarily being regarded as mistaken (or, at least, not mistaken in the sense in which someone who asserted that 'Rome is the capital of France' would be mistaken). In other words, each of the above statements expresses a value judgement to which a warrantable alternative may be offered.

One might therefore suppose that to indoctrinate children with a belief that expresses a value judgement represents an instance of unjustifiable indoctrination, since they will be disposed to reject all counter-instances to it, some of which may be equally commendable. In short, they will not be 'prepared for *variable* calls within certain ranges'. With regard to the fields of aesthetics, politics, and religion, I would agree with this argument. In the moral domain, however, the question of whether it is justifiable to indoctrinate beliefs which express value judgements is more complex. I want to argue that, as far as the child's early moral education is concerned, indoctrinating such beliefs is unavoidable. For example, Derek Wright (1971, p. 158) notes that, according to Piaget: 'the child encounters rules from adults. The source confers a semi-mystical authority upon them; his inability to conceive of other points of view means that once he has accepted the rule into his own thought it cannot be changed or modified'. In other words, children's early moral development begins by their being inducted into the state of mind which I have characterised as 'indoctrinated'. Furthermore, as O'Hear (1981, pp. 123–4) suggests:

> surely, in all subjects, we begin by simply telling children things. Only later do they come to understand the reasons for what they are told, and to accept or reject things for themselves on their own merits. In morality, as in other areas, there is nothing inconsistent or paradoxical in first laying down things that have to be accepted and later leading pupils to see and evaluate the reasons for what they have been told. Indeed, it is hard to see how reasons could be appreciated for what they are unless they were seen as supporting or justifying propositions that were already understood and (provisionally) accepted.

The moral beliefs with which a child is indoctrinated in his/her early years, come under a third category, which I shall call category 'C ' beliefs.

Whether it is justifiable to indoctrinate children with moral beliefs in the later years of their childhood is a difficult question, and one to which I cannot do justice here. Nevertheless, some brief comments are required. It may be that there are certain moral beliefs concerning which we might want older children (and indeed adults) to have closed minds. For example, having attempted to indoctrinate a group of children with a belief such as 'torturing animals is morally wrong', with the result that they accepted the belief, we should not be happy if those children considered that 're-opening the issue [was] a permanent possibility' (Hare 1976, p. 30).

Whether indoctrinating a particular moral belief in this way is warrantable will depend on the arguments which are, or can be, brought forward to support or refute it. These will include considerations such as the non-viability of possible counter-instances to the belief. With regard to beliefs such as 'torturing animals is morally wrong', it may be thought that there are *no* counter-instances which we would wish a child to countenance. Such a belief may therefore be allowed to remain in category 'C' and a teacher can justifiably indoctrinate it. However, it may be desirable to enable children who have achieved a certain level of intellectual maturity to discuss and debate beliefs such as 'one should never steal under any circumstances', since it is the case that warrantable counter-instances to that belief may be offered. Once a decision has been taken by a teacher to proceed in this way, this belief no longer belongs in category 'C'. Rather it must be regarded as a category 'B' belief, with which the children referred to above must no longer be indoctrinated.

Casement (1980) considers that moral education cannot avoid being indoctrinatory. Faced with this, he suggests that we ask a number of questions of any approach to such education. The most important among these are: '"With what beliefs are students indoctrinated?"' and '"How undesirable is it if they are indoctrinated with these beliefs?"' (p. 165). Casement acknowledges that 'there will be disagreement about what constitutes a more undesirable case of indoctrination' (p. 168). However, this 'seems to be something we have to live with. Indoctrination is a complicated matter, and for dealing with it there are no easy answers' (p. 168).

Complacency about the nature of 'indoctrination' and a presumption that it is the preserve of those whose beliefs we do not share, can only lead to the intellectual impoverishment of our children. In concluding this chapter, I suggest that if we see indoctrination in the classroom in terms of the *results* of particular teaching transactions (including reference, where necessary, to the notion of 'influence'), then our perception of 'education' is likely to be altered radically. For now, not only will Communists, Roman Catholics, and pacifists be labelled as 'indoctrinators', but also teachers of mathematics, science and history. The debate will then shift to the discussion of *which sorts* of indoctrination are acceptable. Much of traditional schooling is indoctrinatory, and we must face up to this. It is a testimony to the 'success' of this schooling that many people believe indoctrination to be exemplified in Communism, or pacifism, but not in their own beliefs.

As we have seen, in recent years references to indoctrinatory teaching and its consequences have been all too evident both in the educational and popular press. Three conclusions should, in my view, be drawn from this. The first is that there is a need for teachers and students undertaking teacher education courses to become acquainted with the 'indoctrination debate' and to articulate their own views, perspectives and arguments in regard to it. Secondly, if a teacher's practice is to be impeded by an anxiety that his/her teaching may be labelled 'indoctrinatory', those who would so refer to it have a duty to make clear what *they* understand the term to mean. Finally, if 'indoctrination' is, at least in some sense, unjustifiable, its effects must be countered in the classroom. As I shall argue in the chapters which follow, the teaching of thinking skills is essential to this task.

Note

1. Also included in category 'B' are those beliefs which it is unjustifiable to indoctrinate since they are expressed by propositions which are false. Examples are: 'Oscar Wilde was born in 1859', 'New York is situated on the west coast of the USA', 'the sun revolves around the earth', etc.

Chapter Two

The Education of Young Citizens

In this chapter, I examine the nature and functions of 'education for citizenship' in the early years of schooling. In arguing that the teaching of thinking skills should be regarded as essential to any adequate notion of the term, I consider recent proposals to introduce citizenship into the curricula of schools and discuss in detail one aspect of it: education and cultural diversity.

Education for citizenship

I begin by noting that a concern that schools should provide children with the knowledge, skills, attitudes and dispositions which they will require in order to play a full part as citizens in the society to which they belong and, indeed, in the wider world, is not recent in origin. Over sixty years ago, the Association for Education in Citizenship (AEC) published a volume entitled *Education for Citizenship in Secondary Schools* (1936). In the Preface to the book, the President of the Association, W. H. Hadow, referred to citizenship education as being of 'common and urgent interest' and argued as follows (p. vii):

> Citizenship is the heritage of all of us, and we share the responsibility of bringing it to the highest stage of efficiency which the nature of the subject admits. Some topics, e.g. history, geography, economics, and politics, are immediately germane and relevant; in other cases, such as biology, mathematics, art, and literature, the connexion may be more indirect but the line of approach is equally continuous, and the whole makes up a corpus of Education no branch of which can be safely neglected. The work of the classroom can be strengthened and corroborated by external activities, directed to the one end of inculcating the best kind of life, with as little as possible of bias and partisanship and with the utmost of concentration and dispassionate judgement.

More recently, the authors of *The National Curriculum 5–16: A Consultation Document* (DES/Welsh Office, 1987, para. 4) suggested that 'Since Sir James Callaghan's speech as Prime Minister at Ruskin College in 1976, successive Secretaries of State have aimed to achieve agreement with their partners in the education service on policies for the school curriculum which will develop the potential of all pupils and equip them for the responsibilities of citizenship... in tomorrow's world'. In the late 1980s, an increasing emphasis was placed on the importance of citizenship, allied to calls for a return to 'traditional values'. Indeed, such was the importance given to this theme that several Ministers in the then Conservative Government added their voices in its support. For example, as Home Secretary, Douglas Hurd called for 'lessons in how to be a good citizen... to be made a GCSE exam subject' (Greig 1988). Angela Rumbold, while Minister of State for Education, asked 'the National Curriculum subject working groups to pay attention to cross-curricular themes that [are] "important in ensuring that citizenship and awareness of other people's needs are part and parcel of the lessons which are given to children"' (Hugill and Surkes 1988). At the 1988 Conservative Party conference, Hurd suggested that 'The challenge of the 1990s is to rekindle our strong tradition of citizenship' (Sharrock and Linton 1988); and Kenneth Baker, as Secretary of State for Education, urged the need for 'a moral code in schools to bring back traditional values' (Murphy and Irvine 1988).

As is evident from the AEC quotation given above, the approach advocated by the Association was one which sought to promote citizenship education through subject disciplines. As we enter the new millenium, the idea that schools should prepare children to live as future citizens is once again becoming increasingly prominent and, although the core and foundation subjects of the National Curriculum are important vehicles to encourage this development, the emphasis in recent times has been on much broader conceptions both of the aims and purposes of such education and of how it might be introduced to pupils.

Since the advent of the National Curriculum Council's discussion document *Education for Citizenship* (1990), the relationship between schooling and the formation of citizens has become the subject of keen debate. Although teachers would argue that it has always been part of their responsibility to develop in children an awareness both of the latter's rights within society and their accompanying responsibilities to it, the emergence of 'citizenship' as a cross-curricular theme gave a firm foundation to such work. While a number of books have addressed the nature of 'citizenship' (Barbalet 1988; Jordan 1989; Heater 1990) several have also been published by educationists aiming both to elucidate the notion of 'citizenship education' and to suggest ways in which it might take place in schools (Fogelman 1991; Baglin Jones and Jones 1992; Lynch 1992; Edwards and Fogelman 1993; White 1996).

Two events have contributed to the call for a renewed emphasis on the importance of citizenship education. The first of these was the Archbishop of Canterbury's 'crusade to stop the moral and spiritual decline of the nation' (Thomson and O'Leary 1996, p. 1). Opening a House of Lords debate, the Archbishop argued as follows: 'It would be a failure if our schools were to produce people with the right skills and aptitudes to take on our economic competitors, but who cannot string two sentences together about the meaning and purpose of life or who have no idea what it means to be a good citizen and a moral person' (p. 1). The second concerned the call from Frances Lawrence, widow of the murdered head teacher Philip Lawrence, for 'a national effort to reinforce citizenship and family values, raise the status of authority figures and outlaw violence' (Young 1996, p. 6). In her 'Manifesto for the Nation', Lawrence suggested the need for 'new primary school courses in good citizenship' and 'an emphasis in teaching on effort, earnestness and excellence' (MacAskill and Carvel 1996, p. 1). She argued as follows:

> I would wish to see the emergence of a nationwide movement, dedicated to healing our fractured society, banishing violence, ensuring that the next generation are equipped to be good citizens and urgently debating how the moral climate can be changed for the better... I should like to see lessons in good citizenship begin early in a child's school career. Schools should inculcate an appreciation of the civic bond, the respect we owe to others and the duties we owe to society... I worry that too few people are encouraged to think seriously about the nature and progression of the country... I would hope to encourage an engagement with the important issues, a generation that thinks rigorously about the moral questions behind politics instead of taking refuge in sneering at them (Lawrence 1996, p. 14).

Current proposals for the introduction of citizenship education into schools

In what was referred to as a 'victory' for Mrs Lawrence, the Labour Government indicated its intention to introduce proposals under which children would be taught 'how to be model citizens' (Prescott 1997, p. 1). A White Paper, *Excellence in Schools*, was published in July 1997, in which it was suggested that:

> A modern democratic society depends on the informed and active involvement of all its citizens. Schools can help to ensure that young people feel that they have a stake in our society and the community in which they live by teaching them the nature of democracy and the duties, responsibilities and rights of citizens. This forms part of schools' wider provision for personal and social education, which helps more broadly to give pupils a strong sense of personal responsibility and of their duties towards others. The Department [for Education and Employment] will be setting up an advisory group to discuss citizenship and the teaching of democracy in our schools (DfEE 1997, p. 63).

In the following year, the final report of the Advisory Group on Citizenship, entitled *Education for Citizenship and the Teaching of Democracy in Schools*, was published, under the chairmanship of Bernard Crick (Qualifications and Curriculum Authority (QCA) 1998). The report offers an account of what is referred to as 'effective education for citizenship' which, it is suggested, consists of three elements: social and moral responsibility, community involvement and political literacy. As regards the first of these, the Advisory Group argues that:

> ...guidance on moral values and personal development are essential preconditions of citizenship. Some might regard the whole of primary school education as pre-citizenship,

certainly pre-political; but this is mistaken. Children are already forming through learning and discussion, concepts of fairness, and attitudes to the law, to rules, to decision-making, to authority, to their local environment and social responsibility etc. They are also picking up, whether from school, home or elsewhere, some knowledge of whether they are living in a democracy or not, of what social problems affect them and even what the different pressure groups or parties have to say about them. All this can be encouraged, guided and built upon (pp. 11–12).

The Advisory Group suggests a series of learning outcomes for Key Stages 1 to 4. As the term 'early childhood education' may, at its upper limit, refer to the schooling of children who are eight years of age (Edwards and Knight 1994; Pugh 1996; Blenkin and Kelly 1997), I shall outline the proposals for both Key Stages 1 and 2 (QCA 1998, pp. 46–8):

The learning outcomes for Key Stages 1 and 2

Key Stage 1

Skills and Aptitudes
By the end of Key Stage 1, pupils should be able to:
- express and justify orally a personal opinion relevant to an issue;
- contribute to paired and class discussion on matters of personal and general significance, learning what it means to take turns, respond to the views of others and use acceptable forms of disagreement or challenge;
- work with others and gather their opinions in an attempt to meet a challenge of shared significance;
- use imagination when considering the experience of others;
- reflect on issues of social and moral concern, presented in different ways such as through story, drama, pictures, poetry, and 'real life' incidents;
- take part in a simple debate and vote on an issue.

Knowledge and Understanding
By the end of Key Stage 1, pupils should:
- recognise how the concept of fairness can be applied in a reasoned and reflective way to aspects of their personal and social life;
- understand the different kinds of responsibility that they take on, in helping others, respecting differences or looking after shared property;
- know about the nature and basis of the rules in the classroom, at school and at home; also, whenever possible, know how to frame rules themselves;
- understand that different rules can apply in different contexts and can serve different purposes, including safety, safeguarding of property and the prevention of unacceptable behaviour;
- know about the different kinds of relationships which exist between pupils and between adults and pupils; also have some notion that the power in such

relationships can be exercised responsibly and fairly or irresponsibly and unfairly;

- understand the language used to describe feelings associated with aspects of relationships with others, including words such as *happy, sad, disappointed, angry, upset, shy, embarrassed, peaceful, worried, proud* and *glad;*
- understand different kinds of behaviour using moral categories such as *kind* or *unkind, good* or *bad, right* or *wrong;* know about the consequences of anti-social or egocentric behaviour and attitudes, for individuals and communities; also understand that many problems can be tackled as a community;
- know where they live, in relation to their local and national community, understand that there are different types and groups of people living in their local community such as other children, teenagers, families and old people;
- know about differences and similarities between people in terms of their needs, rights, responsibilities, wants, likes, values and beliefs; also understand that many of these differences are linked with cultural and religious diversity;
- know and understand, through shared activities and the process of exploratory talk, the meaning of key terms such as *respect* or *disrespect, question, comment, discuss, agree* or *disagree, similar* or *different, point of view, opinion, compare and contrast.*

Key Stage 2

Skills and Aptitudes
By the end of Key Stage 2, pupils should be able to:

- express and justify, orally and/or in writing, a personal opinion relevant to an issue;
- contribute to paired and small group discussion on matters of personal and general significance and be prepared to present the outcome to a class;
- work with others in a class and gather their opinions in an attempt to meet a challenge of shared significance through negotiation, accommodation and agreed action;
- use imagination when considering the experience of others and be able to reflect and hypothesise – the 'what if' scenario – on issues of social, moral and political concern in response to stories, drama or 'real life' incidents. These should cover a range of citizenship issues and include consideration of the lives of others living in other places or times and with different values or customs;
- discuss a range of moral dilemmas or problems, in which choices between alternatives are evaluated, selected and justified, using appropriate language;
- participate in a question and answer session in which a member of the local community offers an expert opinion and answers questions prepared in advance by pupils;
- collect information about a topical or contemporary issue from a range of sources, including television and radio news, documentary footage, newspapers

and new communications technologies, and recognise the different ways the sources present the information;
- take part in simple debates and have opportunities to vote on issues.

Knowledge and Understanding

By the end of Key Stage 2, pupils should:
- know at a simple level, how rules and laws are made and the varying purposes they serve; and understand that there are various sources of authority in their duties but that there are also sources of help and support when needed; also understand the meaning of terms such as *rights and responsibilities, right, wrong, fair, unfair, rule, law, forgiveness;*
- understand the need for laws and their enforcement in shaping behaviour and tackling crimes and why certain behaviour is prohibited; also know about the role of the police in the prevention of crime and protection of persons and property, and be aware of the consequences of anti-social behaviour on individuals and communities; also understand the meaning of terms such as *punishment, cause, consequence, justice, fairness, evidence;*
- know about the workings of local and national communities, including the main faiths and ethnic cultures, and how individuals relate to them; know about, in simple terms, contemporary relations between England, Scotland, Wales and Northern Ireland and Europe; know about local and national sources of government and opportunities to participate; also understand the meaning of terms such as *mayor, council, councillor, Member of Parliament (MP), election, vote, parliament, Member of the European Parliament (MEP), political party;*
- understand that there can be different types of government such as democracies and dictatorships; also understand the meaning of terms such as *freedom of speech, opposition, vote, government, King, Queen, Prime Minister, President;*
- know about voluntary and community bodies who work in their local community; also understand the meaning of terms such as *voluntary service, volunteer, charity, protest, petition;*
- know that there are different economic systems; know that there are different ways of allocating scarce resources; understand the choices that have to be made in modern society and the impact on individuals and communities; also understand the meaning of terms such as *fairness, justice, choice, price, services, wealth, market, wage;*
- know about the world as a global community, and that people around the world live in communities as we do; understand that there are similarities and differences between communities in terms of social, economic, cultural, political and environmental circumstances; also understand the meaning of terms such as *poverty, famine, disease, charity, aid, human rights.*

In May 1999, proposals for a review of the National Curriculum in England were published and a public consultation process took place from 13 May until 23 July of that year. The review document includes a framework for personal, social and health education (PSHE) and citizenship at Key Stages 1 to 4, and we are told that: 'The proposals for citizenship build directly from the recommendations in... the final report of the Citizenship Advisory Group' (QCA 1999, p. 13). It is suggested that there should be a joint non-statutory framework for PSHE and citizenship at Key Stages 1 and 2, a non-statutory framework for PSHE at Key Stages 3 and 4, and a programme of study and attainment target for citizenship (which would become a new foundation subject) at Key Stages 3 and 4. If the proposals for citizenship education are acceptable, they would be introduced in September 2002. According to Cassidy (1999, p. 6): 'In the interim, all schools will be expected to follow a broader programme of citizenship and PSHE from September 2000'.

Citizenship education and cultural diversity

As I have mentioned above, there is now an extensive literature on the theory and practice of citizenship education. However, while much of the research which has been published in academic journals has offered general accounts of such education (Carr 1991; Davies 1994; Harris 1995), or particular aspects of it such as education for active citizenship (Wringe 1992), feminist perspectives on education and citizenship (Arnot 1997), global citizenship (Heater 1995; Guin 1996), and democratic citizenship (Park 1997), comparatively little has been written which focuses specifically on the theme of citizenship education and cultural diversity. Notable exceptions are the work of Tomlinson (1992), Gorman (1994) and Sutcliffe and Williams (1999). The latter paper focuses on the murder of the black teenager, Stephen Lawrence, in 1993 and encourages children to think critically about key issues such as: 'duty and care; assuming and checking; identification, information and evidence; background and character; treating people the same and differently; stereotyping; institutions and intentions; prejudice' (pp.33–8).

In 1990, the National Curriculum Council (NCC) suggested that education for citizenship consists of eight components, one of which is 'roles and relationships in a pluralist society'. In a section of its guidance document devoted explicitly to this aspect, the NCC (1990, p. 6) argued as follows:

A democratic society is based on shared values and a variety of cultures and lifestyles can be maintained within the framework of its laws. This component helps pupils to appreciate that all citizens can and must be equal. It increases awareness of and works towards resolving some of the tensions and conflicts that occur between groups which perceive each other to be socially, racially, ethnically or culturally different. In this context, it explores diversity, fairness and justice, cooperation and competition, prejudice and discrimination.

The following areas of study were suggested as possibilities (p. 6):

the interdependence of individuals, groups and communities;
similarities and differences between individuals, groups and communities and their effects;

the existence of differences in perception and the ways in which these may be
reconciled;
Britain as a multicultural, multiethnic, multifaith and multilingual society;
the diversity of cultures in other societies;
a study of history and culture from different perspectives;
international and global issues;
the origins and effects of racial prejudice within British and other societies.

Such areas are useful because they enable children to focus on a number of
problems which they may face at school, in the home and in wider society. A
graphic account of many of these difficulties is set out in *Children and Racism*, a
research study of telephone calls made to ChildLine during the year ending on 31
March, 1995. As the authors note (ChildLine 1996, p. 7):

It is not easy to research the impact of racism. Race and culture are slippery concepts –
they do not have agreed clear definitions. For example, which nation, race or culture do
children of mixed national, cultural or colour inheritance identify with or claim as theirs?
This altogether depends on their relationship to different aspects of their inheritance, and
on how they perceive that these are valued both in general and by those close to them.
It is this very uncertainty in definition, the fluidity of boundaries between so-called
categories, which renders absurd rigidly applied public policies differentiating people in
racial or cultural terms.

In discussing the relationship between citizenship education and cultural diversity,
there are a number of important factors to consider in this study. The first concerns
the fact that 'openly racist harassment and bullying plays a large part in the daily
experience of many black and ethnic minority children' (p. 2). Given this, the notion
of 'citizenship' as an entitlement which accords rights as well as entails responsibilities,
is to some extent a theoretical construct which makes little impact on the lives of many
of those on whom it is, supposedly, conferred. Secondly, the authors suggest that:

there is a generation gap in attitudes, that whether adults want it or not, many young
people are making and will make relationships across cultural, religious and race
frontiers… In resisting this movement, adults create misery and unhappiness for
themselves and their young people, and, in the end, cannot succeed in halting an
unstoppable tide towards new and diverse relationships and identities (p. 3).

The role of citizenship education in focusing on themes such as 'similarities and
differences between individuals, groups and communities and their effects' and 'the
existence of differences in perception and the ways in which these may be
reconciled' is therefore of the utmost importance. As we have seen above, the idea
of 'similarities and differences' has also been referred to extensively by the Advisory
Group on Citizenship. This topic will provide a focus for some of the research
undertaken with young children, which is outlined in Chapter 4.

It is important, at this stage, to consider the following comments made by children in the ChildLine study (pp. 19, 21, 36, 42–3):

I'm bullied at school. They call me 'paki' and shout, 'You don't belong in this country'. Reeta, ten, had written it all in her diary but not yet told anyone. My brother and I are the only Jewish boys at the school. The others call us 'nigger' and 'chocolate biscuit'… I've told my parents and the teachers and they say ignore it… it's really getting me down… I thought of killing myself last week but then I decided not to… You're the only people I can talk to… said David, aged nine.

I have race problems at school and so does my brother. We're picked on all the time. I get punched and kicked and had my head put down the toilet.

I'm going out with a black boy. My parents are Asian. They would go mad if they knew.

I have a black boyfriend. My dad is racist… he's said that if I don't pack him in I can just leave home.

Joanna, 15, was fed up because her parents were Jehovah's witnesses. 'They don't celebrate Christmas… all my friends have a good time and lovely presents… if they send me cards, my parents tear them up.' She had tried telling them she didn't want to be like them and had run away in the past but she was brought back.

I'm finding difficulties with cultural differences… things like going out to discos and even coffee shops are out for me. My parents insist I should be home and studying all the time. I see good things in both cultures. I just don't want to feel under pressure all the time like I do now.

Such views are important not least because children's voices illustrate all too clearly both the complex relationship between 'citizenship' and 'cultural diversity' (Tomlinson 1992; Verma and Pumfrey 1994) and also the fundamental importance of research which seeks to explore topics such as prejudice and prejudice reduction (Aboud 1988; Lynch 1987); 'race' and culture in education (Chivers 1987); 'race' and ethnicity (Gillborn 1990); 'race' and racism (Gill *et al.*1992; Troyna 1993; Gaine 1995; Hewitt 1996); anti-racism, politics and schools (Epstein 1993); children's friendships in culturally diverse classrooms (Deegan 1996); and the role of teacher education in plural societies (Craft 1996).

Citizenship, cultural diversity and international education

Themes such as 'education for citizenship' and 'cultural diversity' feature prominently in approaches to teaching and learning which, for the purposes of this chapter, I shall refer to collectively as 'international education'. These include world studies (Fisher and Hicks 1985; Hicks and Townley 1982; Hicks and Steiner 1989), global education (Pike and Selby 1988; Greig *et al.* 1987; Fountain 1990; Steiner 1996), humane education (Selby 1995), futures education (Hicks 1994; Hicks and Holden 1995), peace education (Hicks 1988) and green education (Randle 1989). Although each of these programmes has a distinctive outlook (Rowley and Toye 1996), they have much in common, sharing similar aims, objectives and approaches to pedagogy.

Fisher and Hicks (1985, p. 8) define world studies as 'studies which promote the knowledge, attitudes and skills that are relevant to living responsibly in a multicultural and interdependent world'. Arguing that world studies can be taught to children of all ages and abilities, the authors give substance to the above definition by suggesting that the subject encompasses:

> (a) studying cultures and countries other than one's own, and the ways in which they are different from, and similar to, one's own; (b) studying major issues which face different countries and cultures, for example those to do with peace and conflict, development, human rights and the environment; (c) studying the ways in which everyday life and experience affect, and are affected by, the wider world (p. 8).

One important reason offered by Fisher and Hicks for teaching world studies is 'learning about others', a theme concerning which they argue as follows:

> The study of 'other people', that is, in countries and cultures other than our own, or at times in history other than our own, helps pupils avoid making false generalisations. These frequently arise from an 'ethnocentric' world view in which people judge others exclusively by their own cultural norms. Learning about others can also help pupils learn about human nature – that is, about themselves (p. 8).

Pike and Selby (1988) offer a detailed list of objectives for global education under the headings 'knowledge', 'skills', and 'attitudes'. The importance accorded to cultural diversity is evidenced by objectives such as:

How others see us: students should learn about their own culture, lifestyles and identities through studying how other people view them.

Prejudice and discrimination: students should understand the nature and workings of prejudice, in themselves and others, and how such prejudices can lead to personal and social discrimination by means of age, class, creed, ethnicity, gender, ideology, language, nationality or race. They should also know about measures to combat discrimination at personal, societal and global levels.

Oppression: students should know about the oppression of groups, in their own and other societies, for reasons of their age, class, creed, ethnicity, gender, ideology, language, nationality or race. They should have an understanding of personal attitudes and social structures which nurture oppression, the part they as individuals play in this process and the contribution each can make towards its diminution.

Diversity: students should be willing to find the beliefs and practices of other cultural and social groups of value and interest, and be prepared to learn from them.

Commonality: students should appreciate the essential worth of others and the commonality of needs, rights, aspirations, behaviour and talents which binds humankind (pp. 63–9).

Susan Fountain's book, *Learning Together: Global Education 4–7* (1990) provides an excellent introduction to the subject for young children. Having asked 'What is global education?', she outlines four 'critical factors': knowledge of interdependence; perspective consciousness; 'state of planet' awareness; and 'awareness of human choices' (pp. 1–3). Responding to the question: 'What do these concepts have to do with young children?' Fountain rejects the view that the latter are incapable of understanding notions such as 'justice', 'rights', 'resource distribution' and 'interdependence'. While it is certainly true that secondary school children are able to grasp such ideas at a more sophisticated level, Fountain argues that: 'in the course of the school day, in their relationships with peers and adults, young children do in fact have simple, concrete experiences which contain elements in common with larger world issues' (p. 3). It is suggested that nursery and infant children frequently:

Call each other names, sometimes gender- or race-related (prejudice); exclude others from play for arbitrary reasons (discrimination); argue over materials (resource distribution); protest that rules are 'not fair' (human rights); fight (peace and conflict); use consumable materials, sometimes unwisely (environmental awareness); find that by sharing and working together, more can be accomplished (interdependence); negotiate to find a solution to a problem that both parties will find acceptable (perspective consciousness); discover that some adults have power in the school to make decisions, or that older children may be allowed to do things that younger ones are not ('state of planet' – or in this case, 'state of school' – awareness); decide what activities they will take part in: write letters, pick up litter, or plant flowers in the school grounds (awareness of human choice and action) (pp. 3–4).

The practical activities which are suggested in each of the three texts referred to above demonstrate, in a very thorough fashion, the extent to which international education can (and should) permeate the curricula of nursery, infant, junior and secondary classrooms. They are stimulating as well as informative and, most importantly, they encourage children (and teachers) to think for themselves. However, one would expect that as international education is orientated towards the discussion and promotion of values, these activities would draw more heavily and systematically upon the explicit teaching of thinking and valuing. When Fisher and Hicks (1985, p. 15) suggest that 'The important goals of world studies teaching… focus on learning to learn, solving problems, clarifying values and making decisions', one wonders why 'learning how to think' has been left out.

Given this, I wish to argue that the teaching of logical and ethical reasoning is essential to any viable conception of 'international education' and of 'education for citizenship'. In short, I suggest, young children should be introduced to philosophical thinking. This stance has been supported by Rowley and Toye (1996) and much excellent work has been undertaken in Britain (Murris 1992; Citizenship Foundation 1992; Rowe and Newton 1994; see also Taylor *et al.* 1998). In addition to the development of such thinking, which is the subject of the next two chapters, I would argue that children also need to acquire proficiency in the skills of argument (see Chapter 6).

At this stage, it is necessary to answer the question: why is the explicit teaching of thinking, reasoning and argument necessary within programmes of international education? In order to do this, I shall focus on *World Studies 8–13: A Teacher's Handbook* (Fisher and Hicks 1985). In a section entitled 'Questions and Values', the authors (p. 18) suggest that:

> If pupils are to grow more aware of their own values and priorities they… should be provided with opportunities [to] choose, prize and act, that is: (a) choose freely; (b) choose from alternatives; (c) choose after thoughtful consideration of the consequences of each alternative; (d) cherish and be happy with their choice; (e) be willing to affirm their choice in front of others; (f) do something as a result of their choice; (g) do this repeatedly, as part of their everyday life.

In evaluating a particular action, children are enjoined to ask themselves three questions: 'Who gains and who loses? Is it wise or unwise? Is it just or unjust?' (p. 18). While Fisher and Hicks are to be commended for encouraging pupils to engage in discussions which require them to clarify and develop their values, nevertheless it is the case that before children can be expected to make informed value judgements they must be able to recognise what, in fact, is to count as a *moral* argument. However, materials promoting a consideration of the nature of morality (a central concern of philosophical thinking skills programmes) are conspicuous by their absence in *World Studies 8–13: A Teacher's Handbook* and in other classroom texts which fall under the banner of 'international education'. Although it is true that some mention is made of the importance of activities involving 'critical thinking' (Fisher and Hicks 1985, p. 25; Huckle 1989, p. 13; Hicks 1994, p. 12) and 'argument' (Huckle 1989, p. 13; Pike and Selby 1988, p. 55), no programme is offered to develop them.

Education for citizenship and the teaching of thinking skills

The important contribution to be made by the teaching of thinking skills to the promotion of cultural diversity is outlined succinctly by Pike and Selby (1988, p. 55):

'It is through [the] interplay between cognitive and affective learning, the analytical and the experiential, learning through reasoned argument and emotional insight, that diversity can be valued yet equality promoted'. In *Education for Citizenship*, the NCC (1990, p. 3) identifies 'arguing a case clearly and concisely' as an important communication skill to be developed through this cross-curricular theme. In addition (p. 4), it is suggested that pupils should 'be helped to develop a personal moral code... to explore values and beliefs' and that they should have 'respect for rational argument'. Schools should provide opportunities for children to:

> compare values and beliefs held by themselves and others and identify common ground;
> examine evidence and opinions and form conclusions;
> discuss differences and resolve conflict;
> discuss and consider solutions to moral dilemmas, personal and social;
> appreciate that distinguishing between right and wrong is not always straightforward;
> appreciate that the individual's values, beliefs and moral codes change over time and are influenced by personal experience (e.g. of the family, friends, the media, school, religion and the cultural background in which an individual is raised) (p. 4).

Finally, the Advisory Group on Citizenship (QCA 1998) makes a number of references to children as critical thinkers:

> It is vital that pupils are provided with structured opportunities to explore actively aspects, issues and events through school and community involvement, case studies, and critical discussions that are challenging and relevant to their lives. It is difficult to conceive of pupils as active citizens if their experience of learning in citizenship education has been predominantly passive (p. 37).

> Certain skills and aptitudes are appropriate to citizenship education. Pupils should have opportunities to develop and apply these skills and aptitudes within pluralist contexts. These contexts should be carefully chosen in order to allow pupils to reinforce and further deepen their understanding, think critically, develop their own ideas, respond in different ways to a diversity of views, defend or change an opinion, and recognise the contribution of others (p. 41).

> The critical reading of newspapers and discussion of television and radio current affairs programmes should be encouraged (p. 42).

I conclude this chapter on a cautionary note. In order to be successful, education for citizenship must do more than merely induct children into certain prevalent modes of behaviour and belief. If this is what is required, the moral educator becomes redundant, since it his/her job to develop those reasoning skills which are a necessary prerequisite for the making of sound moral judgements. Method rather than content should be uppermost in the mind of such an educator. The teacing of thinking skills becomes obsolete when behaviour is the focus of a teacher's attention, simply because successful behaviour modification does not require the person being modified to have developed reasoning abilities at all. Indeed, as all good generals know, an army performs more successfully when the required thinking is undertaken by certain key (and usually senior) personnel.

This observation is relevant in discussing an article by Anthony O'Hear, which has implications for the current debate about the nature and functions of citizenship education. In commenting on the view that such education might involve 'learning about one's civil, political and social entitlements, and about such things as the European Convention on Human Rights', O'Hear (1990, p. 16) argues as follows:

> The free men of Athens who fought for their city and their country at Marathon and at Salamis did not have their heads filled with notions of their entitlements or their armour bursting with charters outlining their rights. They did have a love of their city and its laws and traditions which make them even today models of true citizenship.

He concludes by warning readers that they should be aware of the indoctrinatory possibilities which citizenship education may provide for teachers of different political persuasions.

Once again, it can be shown that adopting a myopic view of 'indoctrination' can seriously damage the credibility of those arguments which are advanced against it. O'Hear fails to note that the Athenian 'models of true citizenship', whom he cites, were themselves a product of indoctrination. This is so precisely because, as O'Hear acknowledges, they lacked the critical, reflective dispositions which he wishes to discredit and which education for citizenship should seek to promote.

I want to argue that teachers cannot concern themselves simply with children's behaviour and the formation of certain fixed beliefs for two reasons. Firstly, it sells pupils short, since it robs them of their intellectual right to think things through for themselves. Secondly, such a policy is unlikely to achieve the goal at which it is aimed (i.e. fostering appropriate but essentially unreasoned conduct). Conformity of behaviour depends upon the overt influence of the teacher, in whose absence a child's actions are likely once more to be regulated by his/her own impulses. Since the code of behaviour (and accompanying beliefs) which were imposed have not been adopted voluntarily by rational means, we must not be surprised if they are rejected by pupils at the first available opportunity. This is why the teaching of thinking skills is essential to education for citizenship.

Chapter 3

Should Young Children be Taught to Think Philosophically?

To date, in Britain, the teaching of philosophy in schools has been advocated against an educational backcloth that has hardly been conducive to its development. As I argued earlier, the advent of the National Curriculum, with its strong emphasis on the acquisition of subject knowledge, its adherence to attainment targets and levels of attainment, and its advocacy of a broad spectrum of study across disciplines, has meant that teachers have had little opportunity to foster an intellectual environment in which critical thinking might flourish in the classroom. Consequently, the discussion of philosophical ideas is a seriously neglected element in the education of young children.

No doubt a major reason for this unfortunate state of affairs is a widespread acceptance of the notion that such children are simply not equal to the task, since they are largely incapable of the mature reflection and rational thought which philosophy presupposes (Levine 1983; Gazzard 1983). Philosophy, it is argued, belongs to the later years of secondary education, if not to universities and colleges. My purpose in this chapter is to suggest that young children should be introduced to philosophical thinking.

Arguments against the teaching of philosophy in schools

Before doing so, the arguments of those who assert that philosophy is for adults and not for children must be countered. This view is by no means recent in origin, having been espoused by both Plato and Aristotle. In the *Republic*, Plato argues that dialectic (philosophy) can only be introduced to those who have completed many years of training and study and who have reached the age of thirty. He suggests that to introduce philosophy at an earlier age is fraught with difficulties:

> And there's one great precaution you can take, which is to stop their getting a taste of [philosophical discussions] too young. You must have noticed how young men, after their first taste of argument, are always contradicting people just for the fun of it; they imitate those whom they hear cross-examining each other, and themselves cross-examine other people, like puppies who love to pull and tear at anyone within reach (1974, Book 7, 539b).

Aristotle argues that the young lack the requisite experience of living to profit from his lectures on politics (to which ethics is a kind of introduction). In their contributions to philosophical discussions, the young merely echo the pronouncements of others. This is in contrast to their ability to become competent in mathematics, the truths of which are derived without recourse to experience:

> One might further ask why it is that a lad may become a mathematician, but not a philosopher or a natural scientist. Probably it is because the former subject deals with abstractions, whereas the principles of the two latter are grasped only as the result of experience; and the young repeat the doctrines of these without actually believing them, but in mathematics the reason why is not hard to see (1976, Book 6, Chapter 8, 1142a, 16–19).

More recently, several well-known professional philosophers have argued against the possible inclusion of philosophy in the curricula of schools. For example, in her book *A Common Policy for Education*, Mary Warnock (1988) suggests that philosophy is properly the preserve of the university undergraduate. Her comments are at times both Platonic and Aristotelian in flavour. To begin with, we are told that philosophy is not 'an appropriate subject for study by pupils at school' (p. 57). Warnock offers the following statement to support this thesis:

> I do not think it possible to study philosophy profitably without entering fairly deeply into the history of the subject, and for this there is not time at school, nor could it be a subject that would interest more than a few pupils. Instant philosophy, philosophy that springs into being in the bath or on the television screen, is fun, but it can hardly be serious (p. 57).

Rather than being introduced to philosophy at school, Warnock suggests that is preferable for pupils to acquire a thorough grounding in and sound understanding of subjects such as mathematics, literature, history and so on, to which the tools of philosophy may be applied at a later date.

What are we to make of Warnock's arguments? It seems to me that they are unconvincing because they contain assumptions which are both unargued and untenable. We need to ask the following questions: (1) In order to engage in philosophy, why is it necessary to enter 'fairly deeply into the history of the subject'? (2) Why should philosophy be thought to be of interest only to a few pupils? (3) Must philosophy be serious to the exclusion of fun?

With regard to the first question, I see no reason to assert that children who are being introduced to philosophy must imbibe, at the same time, a deep knowledge of the history of the discipline. Indeed, I can think of nothing which is more likely to provoke disinterest in the neophyte philosopher than this approach. On the one hand, the pupil is asked to engage in a discussion of ideas which are both new and exciting. On the other, he/she is to be given a history lesson involving a 'roll-call' of famous names accompanied by a résumé of their main texts and theories. This is not to denigrate the importance of the history of philosophy. It is simply to indicate that philosophy is first and foremost an *activity* – it is something one does.

Furthermore, I would suggest, children are fascinated initially by philosophical inquiry precisely because it is so different from anything else which they are offered in the school curriculum. To identify this new subject too closely with a more familiar (and perhaps unpalatable) discipline is to run the risk of the former being rejected by the pupil along with the latter. Protagonists of 'children's philosophy' believe that it is possible (and indeed desirable) to engage in philosophical discussions with young children without requiring them to be imbued with an historical knowledge of the discipline. According to Lipman and Sharp (1979, p. 47):

> Having observed few children eager to browse through Kant or even to peruse the livelier passages of Aristotle, having met with little success in our efforts to convey directly the impact and urgency of the greatest happiness principle, we have been led to draw the irresistible inference that there is an unbridgeable chasm between the disciplined reflection, which is philosophy, and the unbridled wondering characteristic of childhood. It is clear that the plausibility of this inference is now under attack.

Turning to the second question, Warnock offers us no evidence to support her contention that philosophy will be of interest only to a small minority of children. Indeed, the entire history of 'Philosophy for Children', which I shall discuss in the next section, serves to refute this argument. One has only to witness young children discussing philosophical issues to see how keen they are to talk, to debate, to reason, in short, to participate in what Matthew Lipman and his colleagues refer to as a 'community of inquiry' (Lipman *et al.* 1980, p. 45).

On the other hand, the argument that only a few children might become attracted to 'philosophy', as articulated by Warnock, is all too understandable. In her view, whatever else one is doing when one is discussing philosophical issues, one is certainly not having fun! Yet one of the reasons why the children to whom I have taught philosophy over the years looked forward to our sessions is precisely that they enjoyed themselves so much.

In undertaking research for my doctoral thesis (Costello 1990a), I taught philosophy to children in three primary schools. Before concluding my work, I asked children what they thought about our discussions. In response to the statement 'What I like about philosophy is:', I received comments such as: 'You are free to say what you feel about situations'; 'We all do it together. You get a chance to speak'; 'I like the puzzles and the arguments and the discussions'; 'Talking with each other'; 'That it is good listening to other people's verdicts and arguments'; 'Because we don't have to write and I am a slow writer. And we discuss things more and don't just leave it at one answer'; 'Talking about everything around us'.

In arguing for the existence of a dichotomy between those activities which are serious and those which are 'fun', Warnock reminds one of the stern elementary school teacher who demarcated rigidly between 'work' and 'play', and who saw the latter as important only insofar as it enabled children to engage in their studies with renewed vigour. Froebel's epithets 'Play is the child's work' and 'Play is a serious business' should be remembered in the context of this debate. It should be noted that what Warnock offers us is simply her own conception of what the study of philosophy should involve. This view must stand or fall on its ability to compete with alternative conceptions, such as those offered by Lipman and other protagonists of philosophy for (or with) children.[1] Warnock's stand-point is both narrow and restrictive: it encapsulates neither what philosophy can be nor what children can achieve.

At this stage, I would like to offer a brief comment on the views of another professional philosopher, Roger Scruton, who also argues that philosophy should not be taught in schools. In an interview with representatives of the journal *Cogito*, Scruton argues as follows:

> I am against teaching philosophy in schools... It is fine to teach people to question, but first you must give them some certainties. Without certainties the whole point of intellectual endeavour would never be grasped. Unfortunately, and in our time increasingly, school subjects are not being taught as hard fact but as areas of discussion and opinionated vagueness: that is to say, introducing into the classroom issues which can only be understood properly at the level of postgraduate research (Watts-Miller and Whiteside 1988, pp. 3–4).

To this it might be argued that a great many subjects are capable of being understood properly only at postgraduate level. Presumably, however, Scruton would not wish to see them removed from the curricula of primary and secondary schools.

'Philosophy for Children'

Some years ago, in the United States, there emerged what has been called 'a new branch of philosophy' (Lipman and Sharp 1978, p. ix): Philosophy for Children, which has established itself as an important part of the curriculum in American schools and elsewhere. The main pioneer of this new field of philosophy is Matthew Lipman, who was responsible for founding the Institute for the Advancement of Philosophy for Children (IAPC) at Montclair State College (now Montclair State University), in New Jersey.

According to Lipman *et al.* (1980, p. 53), the central aim of Philosophy for Children 'is to help children learn how to think for themselves'. How is this to be accomplished? How are children to be introduced to philosophical thinking? As Minnis *et al.* (1990, p. 43) note:

> Seven novels, with accompanying teachers' manuals, form the core of the Philosophy for Children curriculum. They are designed to foster and expand reasoning skills, beginning in early childhood. Each novel is written for a different age level, beginning with *Elfie*

[for children aged from five to seven years] and ending with *Mark. Elfie, Kio and Gus* and *Pixie* are written for children of primary school age and focus on the meanings of words and their ambiguities… All the children featured have distinct personalities and an individual way of looking at the world.

In *Philosophy in the Classroom*, the following rationale for the novels is given:

The books are works of fiction in which the characters eke out for themselves the laws of reasoning and the discovery of alternative philosophical views that have been presented through the centuries. The method of discovery for each of the children in the novels is dialogue coupled with reflection. This dialogue with peers, with teachers, with parents, grandparents and relatives, alternating with reflections upon what has been said, is the basic vehicle by which the characters in the stories come to learn. And it is how real students likewise come to learn – by talking and thinking things out (Lipman *et al.* 1980, p. 82).

How, then, does Lipman conceive of philosophical discussion taking place in the classroom? A typical session would have the following pattern. First of all, children are asked to read aloud an episode or chapter from one of the novels. According to Fisher (1998, p. 31): 'Poor readers are allowed to "pass" and can choose not to read'. In preparing teachers to teach philosophy, Lipman argues it is necessary that they should be introduced to the novels by reading them aloud in the same way that children are asked to do. As he suggests:

This gives them experience in hearing the language of the text as well as in listening to one another. Taking turns is an exercise in moral reciprocity, and the collective effect of the ensuing discussion is a sharing of the meanings of the text through their appropriation by the group as a whole. Thus, even in the very first stage of exploring the curriculum, the members of the seminar begin to experience themselves as members of a community of shared experience and shared meanings, the first step toward becoming members of a community of inquiry (Lipman 1988, p. 156).

When the designated episode or chapter has been read, children are asked for their comments on it and they have an opportunity to determine which issues are then discussed. The questions asked by teachers, in order to elicit children's responses, will differ according to the age of the latter. For example:

With older students, one might ask, 'What *puzzles* (or perplexes) you about this passage?' so as to focus attention on what is problematic in the subject matter rather than on that which is settled. With younger students, one might ask, 'What *interests* you about this passage?' so as to ensure that questions and comments emerge out of genuine student involvement with the issues. With very young students, these ways of issuing the invitation may be unsuccessful, because small children are unused to being asked for their opinion by adults and may be somewhat bewildered. It is better simply to ask,

'What do you *like* about this paragraph (or page)?' and move from there into the discussion (Lipman 1988, pp. 156–57).

The manuals which accompany the novels contain numerous exercises and discussion plans which will enable both the teacher and the children to focus on those philosophical issues which are raised by the stories. The task of the teacher is to introduce these exercises at an appropriate point in the discussion. Ideally, there should not be slavish adherence to the material contained in the manuals, since this would probably lead to a disregard for those thoughts or ideas which pupils would themselves like to contribute to the dialogue. Neither should there be an undue emphasis on the children's initial comments, as this might result in a failure to address a number of important philosophical issues.

What are the academic, personal and social benefits derived by children who have been introduced to philosophy in the classroom? One excellent account of these is offered by Minnis *et al.* (1990), in a booklet entitled *The Transformers*, which accompanied a BBC television series focusing on 'The Art of Inspired Teaching'. One of the programmes in the series, 'Socrates for Six-Year-Olds', examined the work of Matthew Lipman and the implementation of the 'Philosophy for Children' programme in two schools. In one of these, Tuscan Elementary School, a class of six-year-old children was taught by Catherine McCall, using one of Lipman's novels, *Elfie*.

According to Minnis *et al.*, five months after beginning their philosophy classes with McCall, the children's 'sense of wonder has not diminished, but has been consolidated into serious thinking' (p. 39). Furthermore:

> The children have matured in every way – in concentration, respect for each other, in language – and they are more eager to learn... the children have learnt to ask the right questions, give good reasons and to build on each other's ideas. Children who tended to dominate or have problems concentrating now listen attentively to their classmates, and the reserved children have gained in confidence. According to their teacher, their academic performance has soared ahead. To the core subjects like maths and language, they now confidently bring the same articulate inquisitiveness. By finding their voices in philosophy class, they have become active learners in every sphere (p. 39).

However, one possible difficulty to be overcome by children who are introduced to the IAPC's programme is that philosophy is presented entirely through children's novels. Faced with this, teachers may decide either: (a) to ask pupils to read the stories aloud; or (b) to undertake the reading themselves. In my own teaching, I have always opted for the latter approach. Since in a philosophy class, it is important to find out *what* children think and *why* they think it, I see no reason potentially to alienate poor readers at the outset by requiring that they engage, as a preliminary step to doing philosophy, in an activity in which they have little or no ability.

Of course, it may be claimed that allowing pupils to 'pass' when it is their turn to read offers a solution to this problem. However, I would argue that such a view is fundamentally misguided, since children who feel the need to 'pass' because they are poor readers are unlikely to regard themselves as full participants in the lesson. If this is the case, there is the strong possibility that they will become alienated from an activity (philosophy) in which, given a more appropriate teaching methodology, they may have the potential to demonstrate considerable proficiency. In addition, far from 'solving' the problem of poor readers, such an approach actually exacerbates it, since children are simply provided with one more context, within the school day, where their lack of ability is all too evident (and this is the case whether or not they *attempt* to read the passages in question). These are important points, especially as my own research has shown that some of the most able thinkers are children who are perceived by their teachers to be of below average or low ability as regards reading and writing.

Since the idea of a 'community of inquiry' is central to the IAPC's 'Philosophy for Children' programme, this notion must now be examined. In *Philosophy in the Classroom*, the authors argue that:

> When children are encouraged to think philosophically, the classroom is converted into a community of inquiry. Such a community is committed to procedures of inquiry, to responsible search techniques that presuppose an openness to evidence and to reason. It is assumed that these procedures of the community, when internalised, become the reflective habits of the individual (Lipman *et al.* 1980, p. 45).

Furthermore, we are told that in order to create a community of inquiry certain prerequisites are necessary. There should be a 'readiness to reason, mutual respect (of children towards one another, and of children and teachers towards one another), and an absence of indoctrination' (p. 45). Lipman and his colleagues are only too aware of the problems posed by indoctrination. Indeed, this topic is referred to in various publications written by members of the IAPC. For example:

> There is no study that can more effectively prepare the child to combat indoctrination than philosophy (Lipman *et al.* 1980, p. 85).

> [A philosophical] education is the antithesis of indoctrination as it aims to give children the intellectual tools that they need to think autonomously about moral issues, to explore the metaphysical, logical and aesthetic dimensions of these issues and eventually move toward the formation of their own answers (Sharp 1984, p. 3).

> Non-indoctrinational moral education involves teaching children to engage in ethical inquiry (Lipman 1987, p. 139).

> When philosophy for children is mentioned one occasionally hears the response, 'whose philosophy?' – implying that philosophy is defined as a set of dogmas held by a particular person or group. Perhaps it is this usage that is responsible for fears of indoctrination. It need scarcely be pointed out that philosophy as open inquiry is on the contrary a safeguard against any such danger (Whalley 1987, p. 277).

Two comments must be made about the above quotations. Firstly, each writer conceives of 'indoctrination' as, of necessity, a pejorative term, and consequently as something undesirable which has no place in the classroom. Secondly, the writers are united in their belief that their 'Philosophy for Children' course is non-indoctrinatory. Having already argued at some length against the first contention in Chapter 1, I suggest that the second assertion is mistaken also.

In advancing the view that their programme is not susceptible to the charge of indoctrination, Lipman *et al.* (1980, p. 86) make a distinction between 'procedural' and 'substantive' values. For example, a central tenet of Philosophy for Children is that participants in philosophical discussions should attempt to be 'coherent, consistent, and comprehensive in their thinking' (p. 86). In reply to the criticism that these qualities are simply expressions of personal values, Lipman *et al.* argue as follows:

> coherence, consistency and comprehensiveness are values only in the sense that
> they are standards for effective communication and criteria for effective inquiry. They are
> appropriate to *the way* a person should think, not to *what* he should think. Therefore,
> they are *procedural* considerations, not *substantive* ones (p. 86).

According to the authors, it is only when advocating substantive values that teachers can be accused of indoctrinating their pupils. In rebutting this argument, it should be acknowledged that a number of scholars have sought unsuccessfully to avoid the accusation that their moral education programmes may lead to indoctrinatory outcomes (Wagner 1981). The disclaimers offered by Lipman and his colleagues are also unconvincing. Even if a distinction between procedural and substantive values can be maintained (which is itself a contentious issue), it is possible to show that Lipman's notion of a 'community of inquiry' espouses substantive values. To advocate, as we have seen, a 'readiness to reason, mutual respect... and an absence of indoctrination', is surely to do more than to support 'procedural considerations' (Costello 1990a). Rather than maintaining that it is possible to avoid indoctrination in the moral domain, I would argue that it is preferable to offer open commitment to certain substantive values. To do otherwise, is to fail to appreciate fully the complexity of the concept of 'indoctrination'. A possible consequence of this is that one's views on the moral education of children may fail to be as persuasive as one would wish.

Teaching philosophical thinking in British schools

At the present time in the UK, the teaching of philosophy in schools has become the subject of critical scrutiny. Following the success of Jostein Gaarder's *Sophie's World* (1995), a history of philosophy in the form of a novel, a lengthy article appeared in *The Guardian* entitled 'Laura and Paul do profundity'. In offering a critique both of some of the theoretical perspectives underpinning the teaching of philosophy in schools and of the practices that take place in its name, the author,

Jenny Turner (1996), refers to the work of proponents and critics of such teaching. As regards the latter, Turner interviewed John White of the Institute of Education, University of London, whom she reported to have said the following (p. 26):

> Obviously we want people to learn to think. And this stuff is certainly attention-grabbing and I daresay there are good things about it, but it isn't really philosophy. For it to be philosophy, [the children would] have to move on from simple questions and arguments to more complex and sustained ones. And I've never seen any evidence that they do.

In his 'The roots of philosophy' (1992), White examines the claims of those he refers to as 'enthusiasts for children's philosophising' (p. 74). In doing so, he suggests:

> We need, first, to test whether the accounts that theorists give of what children do match the facts. A first issue here is whether children in fact say what they are alleged to say. *Do* young children typically – or indeed ever – ask 'What are possibilities?' 'What is my identity?' 'What's value?'? Since we are given no further evidence we cannot judge, but it is rather hard to swallow (p. 74).

White also raises a second issue of concern, namely 'whether the descriptions theorists give of what children say are always well-grounded' (p. 74).

An important question must now be answered: how can supporters of children's philosophy convince the sceptic that what is taking place in the classroom is genuinely philosophical? In a review of Michael Pritchard's book, *Philosophical Adventures with Children* (1985), Miller attempts to counter the most potent criticism which has been made of the 'Philosophy for Children' movement, namely that it fails to refute the popular view that 'children are utterly incapable of real philosophical thinking' (1986, p. 46). In order to do this, he catalogues the means by which advocates of Lipman's 'Philosophy for Children' programme can seek to convince others that they are successful in enhancing philosophical thought in their students. He suggests that:

> Previous evidence for the success of the programme can be roughly divided into
> three categories: (1) the testimony of those who have used the programme, (2) tapes and transcripts of actual sessions, (3) the results of objective tests [undertaken] by children exposed to the programme (p. 46).

Miller discusses the third category only briefly, since, as he says, there are no objective tests to assess the quality of philosophical reasoning. A number of tests in other subjects, e.g. reading, mathematics and critical reasoning, may be offered to children, both before and after they have studied philosophy, in order to indicate the extent to which this study has improved their performance in other academic subjects. However, such tests tell us little about children's progress in philosophy itself. The obvious difficulty with teachers' testimony as a means of demonstrating children's philosophical ability is, as Miller recognises, that such testimony can be based on selective bias. This may be true inasmuch as teachers, either wittingly or unwittingly, succumb to the temptation to include only that evidence which is conducive to the fulfilment of their expectations. Indeed, in the absence of further proof, teachers become susceptible to the charge that many, if not all, of their findings are, at least, exaggerated. Consequently, it is incumbent on protagonists of children's philosophy to offer substantial transcripts of taped discussions. Such an approach is important for two reasons. Firstly, it demonstrates that the dialogues actually took place. Secondly, the difficulties associated with selective bias are minimized. They may not be avoided completely, since it is possible, and indeed necessary, to offer transcripts of selected audio- or videotapes. To circumvent this problem, the researcher should be expected to provide a selection of children's dialogues.

One familiar problem remains. This concerns the possibility that, having examined the transcript of a philosophical discussion, the sceptic may simply dismiss it as 'children talking'. In other words, the philosophical nature of many of the comments made may pass unnoticed. As Miller points out: 'Pritchard is well aware of the probability that someone who does not quite know what to look for, and/or doesn't want to see it, will not find genuine philosophical insights in the children's conversations without help' (p. 47). In order to provide assistance in this matter, Pritchard punctuates children's dialogues with his own commentaries, indicating where philosophical problems are being examined. Thus, it becomes extremely difficult for the sceptic to assert that the subject matter of philosophy is not central to the discussions. Miller's comment is apposite here:

> A sceptic could be exposed to examples of good philosophical discussions by children and come away unconvinced. She could fail to see the philosophical content of an actual conversation due to her own prejudice and/or lack of training... By providing plenty of commentary Pritchard minimised the likelihood that the philosophical content of the transcripts he reproduced will not be seen (p. 47).

This is the approach which I have adopted in undertaking my previous research in primary schools. In so doing, my aim has been to suggest that the disdain shown by some professional philosophers towards what takes place in the classroom in the name of 'philosophy' is unwarranted. Annotating dialogues should ensure that readers are able to judge how proponents of children's philosophising themselves view the work presented, in terms of its content and quality. If, as a result of this rigorous approach, differing perspectives are articulated concerning whether or not what is taking place in schools is genuinely philosophical, then at least the debate will be well informed by the evidence that has been gathered.

The best way to refute arguments against the teaching of philosophy in schools is to show in some detail that children are able to engage, in a competent fashion, in philosophical debate and argument. This I have demonstrated elsewhere, in the context of the primary school (Costello 1990a, 1993a, 1993b, 1995a, 1996a). My own approach conceives of philosophy being taught in three ways. Firstly, children's short stories can be used as vehicles for the introduction of philosophical ideas. I have written a number of such stories involving three children: Knowlittle, Knowless and Knownothing. These characters inhabit a fantasy world, making visits to the Snow Queendom, and to the kingdoms of King Extrawork and King Eversonice etc., in the search for a domain where there are some good rules by which to live (see Appendix 1).

With regard to storytelling, such a setting creates the maximum potential for the writing of stories which are capable of capturing children's attention and interest. Once this has been achieved, the philosophical themes which are embedded in the text can be discussed more readily. I also include here a transcript of a discussion in which I engaged with a class of eight- to eleven-year-old children concerning one of these stories (Costello 1988a; see Appendix 2).

To do so is important for four reasons. Firstly, the dialogue illustrates pupils' willingness and ability to think critically about philosophical issues. Secondly, some of the most able speakers in the discussion were among the youngest in the class. Thirdly, in Chapters 4, 5 and 6, I examine several discussions conducted with children at Key Stage 1. With this in mind, it is important for teachers to have a sound understanding of the continuity which exists between the key stages, in order to ensure optimum development of children's thinking skills. Finally, the dialogue demonstrates that philosophy provides an ideal means by which teachers may encourage pupils to articulate views, express arguments and reflect on their own thinking and that of others.

The importance of fantasy in the lives of young children has been argued for by a number of scholars. Perhaps the best known of these is Bruno Bettelheim, whose celebrated book, *The Uses of Enchantment*, is aptly subtitled: *The Meaning and Importance of Fairy Tales* (1976). In discussing the importance of children's stories, Bettelheim declares that: 'For a story truly to hold the child's attention, it must entertain him and arouse his curiosity. But to enrich his life, it must stimulate his imagination; help him to develop his intellect and to clarify his emotions' (p. 5). According to Bettelheim, fairy tales are the most appropriate medium through which to accomplish these goals. It is true, he argues, that:

> on an overt level fairy tales teach little about the specific conditions of life in modern mass society; these tales were created long before it came into being. But more can be learned from them about the inner problems of human beings, and of the right solutions to their predicaments in any society, than from any other type of story within a child's comprehension (p. 5).

In suggesting that children find fairy stories more appealing than other kinds of children's literature, Bettelheim believes that this is because such stories 'in a much deeper sense than any other reading material, start where the child really is in his psychological and emotional being' (p. 6).

A second method of engaging children in philosophical reflection is to offer them samples of reasoning (embedded in logical, ethical and more general philosophical problems) to discuss (Costello 1988b, 1989a, 1990a). Finally, diagrammatic representation (e.g. overhead projector transparencies) may be used to initiate discussions. This is particularly important for children who are poor readers but whose reasoning ability may be as good as, or better than, that of their peers (Costello 1988b, 1989a, 1990a).

Before concluding this chapter, I wish to return to the views of those (professional philosophers and others) who have suggested that the introduction of young children to philosophical thinking in schools is problematic. In Chapter 2, I argued that the teaching of critical thinking skills should be regarded as essential to any viable conception of 'education for citizenship'. In order to facilitate such teaching, several non-IAPC programmes have been advanced which focus on the development of philosophical and moral reasoning (Murris 1992; Citizenship Foundation 1992, Rowe and Newton 1994). For example, 136 primary schools trialled the Citizenship Foundation's manual of teaching activities which was produced as part of its Primary Citizenship Project and which encouraged children to discuss questions such as:

> Is it a good thing for people to trust people in charge of them?
> Why do people obey orders?
> Do people have to do as they are told?
> What do we need to know to be sure about something?
> What makes people brave?
> What makes a punishment fair?
> Is it ever right to steal? (Citizenship Foundation 1992, pp. 13–15).

As is evident from this series of questions, the topics which children are asked to debate are genuinely philosophical and feature prominently, for example, in undergraduate philosophy courses. Of course, those who are opposed to the notion of 'children's philosophy' as a vehicle for teaching critical thinking skills will suggest that the discussions which take place in primary classrooms on the nature of courage, fairness, authority and morality, are very different from those which are the norm in undergraduate seminars. While this is certainly true, I am not sure what advocates of such an argument believe has been achieved by gaining this admission. Are they suggesting that, because philosophical discussions conducted by eight-year-olds tend to be less sophisticated than those of nineteen-year-olds studying philosophy, the former ought to be abandoned? If this is the case, then the rationale for primary school mathematics, history, science and so on is also undermined. Since it is absurd to suggest that one could begin the study of such subjects at undergraduate level, why is it often presumed, by professional philosophers and others, that philosophy is an exception in this respect?

I suggest that there are three reasons for this. The first concerns the view that philosophy is a rather difficult subject to study. This perception has been enhanced by the fact that philosophical problems neither die nor fade away – they remain unsolved and ever-beguiling despite the persistent attention of some of history's greatest minds. Consequently, philosophers tend to stress the need for experience of life as an important requirement before systematic reflection on philosophical problems can take place. As children have little such experience, so the argument goes, they are to be excluded from the enterprise.

The second reason, which focuses on the nature of philosophical literature, is related to the first. Here the argument is that such literature is clearly beyond the understanding of young children and therefore they are ill-equipped to discuss philosophical topics. However, while the premise of this argument may be true, the conclusion certainly does not follow from it. As Lipman and Sharp (1979, pp. 47-48) have argued:

> ... there are ways of engaging children in philosophical activities long before they are competent to read anything in the traditional philosophical repertoire. The paradoxes of appearance and reality, permanence and change, unity and diversity, are enchanting to them from early childhood, perhaps a decade or two before they are prepared to tackle Heraclitus or Parmenides... Children for whom the formal presentations of philosophy are anathema may find hints of the same ideas entrancing when embedded in the vehicle of a children's story.

The third reason is political – professional philosophers simply want to be the first to introduce young people to their discipline. As philosophy is very different from most other subjects which students have encountered during their schooling, this introduction is likely to be significant for many of them. Being taught, perhaps for the first time, *how* rather than *what* to think is an exhilarating experience. Not unnaturally, philosophers are keen to be responsible for such educational development themselves.

In my view, none of the reasons outlined above is sufficient to warrant the exclusion of young children from the discussion of philosophical problems. Indeed, I would argue that exposure to the skills of critical thinking and reasoning at an early age is essential if children are to cultivate those reflective habits which are crucial to their future lives as citizens in a democracy. To begin this process only at a university or other higher education institution is to arrest children's intellectual development and to imply that 'education for citizenship' is simply an exercise in indoctrination.

Omitting to offer children explicit teaching which is aimed at fostering their thinking and valuing processes, may have serious implications for their academic achievement. For example, we might ask why it is that children who enter school at four or five years of age questioning many things, often emerge from a period of compulsory schooling questioning very little (Martens 1982). One consequence of limiting the study of philosophy to secondary schools, colleges and universities, is that the thought processes of students will already have been formed by the time an introduction to critical thinking becomes possible (Lipman, in Roddy 1981, p. 6). According to Levine (1983 p. 5), such thought processes are 'the standard constructs of the social community'.

So my response to the question with which I began this chapter is an unequivocal 'Yes'. Philosophical training must be given to children at an early age, since without it they will merely appropriate the standard (and often unreasoned) beliefs and opinions prevalent in their immediate environment. The teaching of philosophy to children can do much to counteract the prejudices and uncritical thinking which are a fact of everyday adult life. It is the responsibility of the philosopher, one of whose tasks is to clarify our thinking, to initiate such teaching.

Note
  1. The term 'Philosophy for Children' refers to the teaching programme devised by Matthew Lipman and his colleagues at the IAPC; 'philosophy with children' refers to other (non-IAPC) programmes and approaches to teaching and learning in this field.

Chapter 4

Developing Philosophical Thinking in the Early Years Classroom

In this chapter, I examine a research project which I undertook in two infant schools together with a colleague, Maggie Bowen. Having discussed key issues which underpinned the project, I evaluate a dialogue which took place with a class of six- to seven-year-old children.

Teaching thinking skills through the medium of video

As I said in Chapter 3, my previous research took place in primary schools using three media: stories written for children, samples of reasoning, and diagrammatic representation. In setting out to explore the nature and quality of pupils' thinking in the early years of their education, I decided to focus exclusively on videotapes as a pedagogic resource. In *Teaching Philosophy with Picture Books*, Murris (1992) outlines her own very successful programme for developing young children's thinking skills, of which the video presentation is an important element. Furthermore, a substantial amount of research has now taken place which demonstrates the positive impact which the *Sesame Street* television series has had on children's academic, personal and social development (Ball and Bogatz 1970; Bogatz and Ball 1971; Children's Television Workshop/Educational Testing Service 1990; Wright and Huston 1995).

The two schools which took part in the research are members of the North East Wales Institute's partnership scheme for initial teacher education courses. As good working relationships had already been established between the schools and one of the researchers, the former were enthusiastic participants in the project. For the purposes of the discussion which follows here and in Chapter 5, the schools will be referred to as 'School A' and 'School B' respectively. In School A, the researchers worked with one class of 25 five- to six-year-old pupils (hereinafter referred to as Class A), while in School B, two classes of children, aged six-to-seven years were the focus of the research. These latter classes (hereinafter referred to as 'Class B1' and 'Class B2'), contained 17 and 22 pupils respectively.

No attempt to draw comparisons (between either the two schools or the two classes in School B) was made; indeed, this was not an aim of the project. Rather, our essential goals, as educational researchers, were: (1) to assess the extent to which children at Key Stage 1 are capable of thinking critically, reasoning soundly and arguing cogently, and, if such abilities can be demonstrated (2) to offer recommendations as to how the teaching of thinking skills might be facilitated in the early years classroom. The following dialogue, which took place with Class B2, involves both the discussion of school rules and of the concepts 'same' and 'different'.

Developing children's philosophical thinking

MB	The first thing we are going to do today is talk about rules. Now I know from talking to [head teacher] that you do have some school rules that you have to try and keep. So can anybody tell me some of the rules that you've got at school? Shani?
Comment	*As we saw in Chapter 2, the Advisory Group on Citizenship suggested that 'By the end of Key Stage 1, pupils should... know about the nature and basis of the rules in the classroom, at school and at home' (QCA 1998, p. 46).*
Shani	'Please' and 'Thank you'.
MB	Say 'Please' and 'Thank you'. Zack?
Zack	Don't fight.
MB	Don't fight. Shauni?
Shauni	Don't break windows.
MB	Don't break windows. Yes, good girl. Kaylee?
Kaylee	Be polite.
MB	Be polite. Nathan?
Nathan	Be nice and be fair.
MB	Be nice and be fair – that's a nice one. Jonathan?
Jonathan	Don't write on people's walls – on the school walls.
MB	Good. Gareth?
Gareth	Don't disturb the teachers.
MB	Don't disturb the teachers when they're working. Scott?
Scott	Don't throw stones at cars.
MB	Don't throw stones at cars – that's a good rule isn't it? You mustn't do that when the cars come into the school playground? Jason?
Jason	Don't throw food around.
MB	Don't throw food around. Michaela?
Michaela	Don't smash into the school yard and smash windows.
MB	Amy?
Amy	Don't shout at the teachers.
MB	Alisha?
Alisha	Don't throw things at cars.
MB	Don't throw things at cars. Dakota?

Dakota	Don't vandalise.
MB	Don't vandalise. That's another good school rule. Zack?
Zack	Don't pull tongues.
MB	Don't pull tongues at each other. Jason?
Jason	Don't throw fruit at cars.
MB	Don't throw fruit at cars. Gareth?
Gareth	Don't let dogs in the playground.
MB	You don't let dogs in the playground – they might make a mess mightn't they?
Alex	Don't write on other people's work.
MB	Don't write on other people's work. Nathan?
Nathan	Listen carefully.
MB	Listen carefully. Good boy.
Kirsty	Be fair.
MB	Be fair. We'll have one more and then I'll…
Ryan	I've got a good one.
MB	You've got a good one – O.K.
Ryan	Don't break branches off the trees.
MB	Don't break the branches off the trees.
——	Don't drop litter.
MB	Michaela?
Michaela	Don't punch and kick.
MB	Don't punch and kick. Zack? One more now.
Zack	Don't throw things at vehicles.
MB	Don't throw things at vehicles – O.K. Now then, outside in the corridor, I see three rules and those three rules are: 'Help each other'; 'Be sensible'; and 'Do your best'. Now the first one, 'Help each other', can anybody tell me what that means? What does that rule mean? Leanne?
Comment	*An important task of philosophy is to clarify both the meaning and use of words or concepts. In order to enhance children's linguistic competence and their critical thinking skills, questions such as 'What does X mean?' and 'What do you mean by…?' should be asked frequently in all curriculum areas.*
Leanne	Don't be nasty to each other.
MB	Samantha?
Samantha	If someone's stuck, you can help them.
MB	Amy?
Amy	If someone fell over, help them.
——	That's what I was going to say.
MB	Dakota?
Dakota	I forgot because I was going to say what Amy said.

MB	O.K. Zack?
Zack	If someone got a nosebleed, give them a tissue.
MB	That's lovely, yes, good boy. Ryan?
Ryan	If someone falls over, take them to the teacher.
MB	That's a nice way of helping somebody. Nathan?
Nathan	If they haven't got much food, share it.
MB	That's very nice – if they haven't got much food, share it. Shauni?
Shauni	Share your things.
MB	Share your things. Michaela?
Michaela	My mum is getting clothes ready for Kosovo.

Comment   *Comments such as this, which young children make spontaneously and without prompting, demonstrate their developing global awareness and the importance of promoting 'the knowledge, attitudes and skills that are relevant to living responsibly in a multicultural and interdependent world' (Fisher and Hicks 1985, p. 8). This is an essential aim of international education (see Chapter 2).*

MB	Is she? That's a nice way of helping somebody, isn't it? A lovely way of helping. Oh Dakota, you remembered.
Dakota	Be kind to your friends.
MB	Be kind to your friends. Let's think about 'Be sensible'. What does that mean? Scott?
Scott	I forgot.
MB	You forgot. Gareth?
Gareth	Be good.
MB	Be good. Jonathan?
Jonathan	If someone says: 'Smash a window' or something bad, you just say 'No'.
MB	Because that wouldn't be sensible to smash a window, good boy. Shauni?
Shauni	If someone tells you to do something bad, you don't do it.
MB	Good girl… Nathan?
Nathan	Be brave to say 'No'.
MB	Be brave to say 'No'. Good boy. Aimee?
Aimee	Be good.
MB	Be good. That's very sensible, isn't it? Michaela?
Michaela	P.C. [name] told us not to say no…um…yes to help him.
——	Don't keep secrets.
MB	That's what the policeman who came to school told you, did he?
Nathan	The policeman said if there's any strangers and you don't know them, and they ask you if you want a sweet or something, you should say 'No'.

Comment	*Encouraging children to converse in this way offers the opportunity for a dialogue to explore several (often quite different) topics – in this case, pupils' safety.*

MB	That's right – that's sensible, isn't it? … Zack?
Zack	Don't chuck stones at car windows.
MB	Right. That's not a very sensible thing to do, is it? Jason?
Jason	Say 'Please' and 'Thank you'.
MB	Say 'Please' and 'Thank you'.
Shauni	Don't wander off.
MB	Do you want to tell me about being sensible, Amy?
Amy	Don't be silly.
MB	Don't be silly. Gareth? Last one.
Gareth	Don't push people.
MB	Don't push people. What about the last rule I've seen in your school: 'Do your best'. What does that mean?
Alisha	Try hard.
MB	Try hard. Amy?
Amy	Don't give up.
MB	Michaela?
Michaela	Do your work nicely.
MB	Do your work nicely. Scott?
Scott	Do work hard.
MB	Do work hard. Shani?
Shani	Try your best on your work.
MB	Zack?
Zack	Do your best on the gardening.
MB	Do you help do the gardening in school sometimes?
Zack	No, at home.
MB	Good. Jonathan?
Jonathan	If you can't do your work, just try your best and you might be able to do it.
MB	Great. Shauni?
Shauni	Don't stop trying.
MB	Don't stop trying. Jason?
Jason	Try and not have a day off.
MB	Try and not have a day off. Dakota?
Dakota	Try hard – try to get a sticker or a sweet.
MB	Natasha?
Natasha	Listen to the teacher before you do your work.
MB	Any more for 'Do your best'?
Alisha	Listen to the teacher.
MB	Listen to the teacher. Nathan? Last one. What does 'Do your best' mean?

Comment	*Requests to clarify meaning are made on several occasions during this dialogue.*
Nathan	If you go to the gymnastics club, like we did last time, then if she says 'Stay by here', you should stay by here because there is busy roads and you could get knocked over by a car, and the teacher would be in trouble.
MB	Now then, let's think about those rules again: 'Help each other'; 'Be sensible'; 'Do your best'. I want you to tell me which you think is the most important rule… and why. So get Ernie and we'll pass him round to you first, Dakota. Which do you think is the most important rule?

Comment	*An Ernie puppet was used during some of the lessons, when children were asked for their views on a particular topic. They were told that if they did not have a comment to make, they could simply pass Ernie to the person sitting next to them. This approach obviates the need to say 'Pass' and, as a silent affirmation of the wish not to speak, reduces the possibility of embarrassment on the part of pupils. Furthermore, they were told that when someone was holding Ernie, it was very important for other members of the group to listen carefully to what was being said. An appropriate emphasis on the importance of both speaking and listening is essential to the success of a thinking skills programme.*

Dakota	Listen to your teacher and help your teacher when she feels sad.
Helen	Help your teacher and try your best.
Alisha	Help each other when people fall over.
Aimee	Help each other.
Natasha	Do your best on everything.
Martin	Help your friend when they're stuck on something.
Samantha	Help the teacher because she works hard.
Leanne	Help the teacher because she works hard.
Michaela	Help the teacher because she gives us good work.
MB	Right, let's go over the rules again: 'Help each other'; 'Be sensible'; 'Do your best'. Which do you think is most important?

Comment	*Here an attempt is made to focus children's minds on the question first asked of Dakota above: 'Which do you think is the most important rule?' One important feature of this dialogue (and those which follow in Chapter 5 and Appendices 3 and 4) is repetition by the teacher, both of key ideas, themes or questions and of pupils' individual comments. This is important in helping children to develop an understanding of the topic being discussed.*

Emina	Help your teacher and be good.
Kaylee	Help your teacher and be sensible.
Nathan	Be sensible and listen to your teacher when you're spoken to.
Liam	Don't throw stones at cars.
Jonathan	When someone's lonely or hasn't got much food, share and be kind.
Alex	Help each other and be good.
Gareth	Don't throw stones at windows, because if someone's there, you might hit them.
Scott	Be polite.
Shani	Help children if they're sad.
Zack	Don't chuck stones at vehicles.
Jason	Don't break things.
Ryan	Be fair.

Comment   *Ryan invites a discussion of the concept of 'fairness'.*

Shauni	Share.
MB	Some of you have mentioned about being fair. What does 'being fair' mean, Shauni?

Comment   *The Advisory Group on Citizenship suggested that 'By the end of Key Stage 1, pupils should recognise how the concept of fairness can be applied in a reasoned and reflective way to aspects of their personal and social life' (QCA 1998, p. 46).*

Shauni	Be kind.
MB	Be kind, yes. Kaylee, what does 'being fair' mean?
Kaylee	Giving someone your sweets.
MB	Michaela?
Michaela	If you've got stickers, share them.
MB	Dakota?
Dakota	Share other things.
MB	Zack?
Zack	Share your sweets with people.
MB	That's fair, isn't it? Michaela?
Michaela	Share your toys.
MB	O.K. Last one.
Aimee	Don't be nasty.
MB	Now we are going to do something different – something completely different. What does the word 'different' mean? Zack?

Comment   *The lesson now progresses to a discussion of the terms 'same' and 'different'. As we saw in Chapter 2, these are referred to by the Advisory Group on Citizenship and by authors writing on the subject of international education. These concepts are also frequently the subject of philosophical discussion. Indeed,* Thinking: The Journal of Philosophy for Children *offers two articles which focus on the relationships between them: one is written by a philosopher (Crawshay-Williams 1986), while the other is an account of a dialogue which took place with primary school pupils (Gazzard 1986).*

Zack	That it is different from something.
MB	Right, good boy. Jonathan?
Jonathan	If you're doing mathematics, you're going to do something different, you're going to do handwriting.
MB	Jason?
Jason	Black and red are different.
MB	That's right. Shauni?
Shauni	Different colour people.
MB	Different coloured people, good girl. Scott?
Scott	Green and yellow.
MB	Green and yellow are different. Liam?
Liam	Different colour hair.
MB	Michaela – last one.
Michaela	If you're doing R.E. and you want to do something else, you could do 'Mousematics'.
MB	And that would be different. Shani?
Shani	Red and yellow are different.
MB	So now for something different and a different person's voice to listen to.
PC	Now we've just talked a little bit about what 'different' means. Who can tell me what the word 'same' means? Zack?
Zack	You look the same as it.
PC	You look the same as…
Zack	Some friends of yours.
PC	Good boy. Jonathan?
Jonathan	Like this chair and that chair – it's the same.
PC	Very good. Nathan?
Nathan	Some people have got the same coloured hair.
PC	Some people have got the same coloured hair. Amy?
Amy	Red and red are the same.
PC	Red and red are the same.
Dakota	We're not the same outside, but we're the same inside.

Comment   *Dakota's comment raises the philosophical problem of personal identity. For a discussion of this topic with primary school pupils, see Costello (1995a).*

PC	What does that mean? That's a very interesting statement. Could you say that again, Dakota?
Dakota	We're different outside but we're the same inside.
PC	Who can tell me what that statement means? We're different outside but the same inside. Alisha?
Nathan	It means that we're… Some people who've been in hot countries are a different colour; they're not the same as us, because we are not in that hot country, and inside we've got the same skeletons.

Comment   *Nathan suggests that, in contrast to skin colour, bone structure is one aspect of personal identity which human beings have in common.*

PC	That's an excellent explanation, Nathan. Amy?
Amy	That we all share.
PC	That we all…
Amy	Share.
PC	What do we share? We all share what? Michaela?
Michaela	Toys and sweets.
PC	We share toys and sweets. What else do we share? Shani?
Shani	I wanted to say 'Sweets'.
PC	Oh, you were going to say the same as Michaela. Shauni?
Shauni	We share everything that we have.
PC	O.K. We share everything that we have. Jason?
Jason	We share food.
Ryan	We share our money.
Gareth	We share drinks.
PC	Jonathan?
Jonathan	If I have a drink at my house, I will give my friend a drink as well.
PC	Why would you do that?
Jonathan	Because if I'm playing with my friend, it wouldn't be fair on my friend if I had a drink and my friend doesn't.
PC	Now, you've raised some very important issues. And the next thing we're going to do is talk a little bit more about this word 'same' and the word 'different'. And what I am going to ask you to do now is to look at the person sitting next to you… and think about one thing that is the same about you both and one thing that is different. This is how we are going to do it… Just look at each other's faces, that would be a good way to start.

PC divides the class into groups of two or three. Children talk to each other for two minutes.

PC	Right, now let's think about some of these things that are the same and that are different. I'll start over here. Now, Dakota, I want you to think about one thing that is the same between you and Helen.
Dakota	We've got the same eyes – colour eyes.
PC	What colour are your eyes?
Dakota	Blue.
PC	That's excellent. Now Helen, could you tell us one thing that's different between you and Dakota?

Helen does not reply.

PC	O.K., I'll come back to you – have a think about it. Alisha, can you tell me one thing that is different between you and Amy?
Alisha	We've got different names.
PC	Now, Natasha, could you think of one thing that is the same between you and Aimee?

Natasha does not reply.

PC	Can anybody think of something that's the same between Natasha and Aimee? Jonathan is a star this morning.
Jonathan	They've got the same colour tongue.
PC	That's very interesting, isn't it? And what colour would that be?
Jonathan	Red.

Some children say 'Pink' and others say 'Red'.

PC	O.K. Now, Martin and Samantha. Samantha, can you tell me one thing that's the same between you and Martin?
—	Same colour hair.
PC	Emina, can you think of one thing that's the same between Martin and Samantha?
Emina	They've got the same legs.
PC	They've got the same legs… Michaela?
Michaela	They've got the same socks.
PC	We can't see Martin's socks, can we? Now Leanne and Michaela: one thing that's the same between you two.
Michaela	We've got the same socks on.
PC	One thing that's different, Leanne?
Leanne	We haven't got the same clothes on.
PC	You haven't got the same clothes on. Can you tell me one piece of clothing that's different?
Leanne	The dress.
PC	Why is the dress different?

Leanne	Because I haven't got a dress on.
PC	Excellent. Now Emina and Kaylee. One thing that's the same, Emina?
Emina	We've got the same colour hair.
PC	And one thing that's different, Kaylee?
Kaylee	We've got different shoes.
PC	You've got different shoes, very good. Now Nathan and Liam and Jonathan. Now Liam, tell me one thing that's different between you and Nathan.
Liam	He's got a green top and I've got a blue top.
PC	Excellent. Now can you think of one thing, Jonathan, that's the same between you and Liam?
Jonathan	We've both got black shoes.
PC	Now we've got Alex and Gareth. Gareth, can you tell me one thing that's different between you and Alex?
Gareth	He's got green eyes, I've got brown eyes.
PC	Alex, one thing that's the same between you two.
Alex	We're the same inside.
PC	Now in what sort of ways do you think you are the same inside?
Alex	Our bones.
PC	Any other ways that you are the same inside?
Michaela	Blood.
PC	Good girl. Now this is an interesting question I've got for Alex and everyone can have a think about it. How do we know, Alex, that we are the same inside? How do we know that?
Comment	*Together with 'What do you mean?', one of the most fundamental philosophical questions is 'How do you know?' Indeed an entire branch of philosophy, epistemology, is devoted to a consideration of issues associated with the latter (see Scruton 1997).*
Alex	By X-rays.
PC	Oh, that's super! One way of being able to tell is doctors can perform X-rays on us. Do we have any other ways, Nathan?
Nathan	If there's two people at the same time having an X-ray, and there's two doctors and they both have an X-ray, and then if you look at the two screens where the X-ray shows all your bones, they'll be the same bones.
PC	That's a super explanation. Jonathan, one more on this. How do we know that we are the same inside?
Jonathan	Because sometimes you can see through your skin and you can see what's there sometimes.
PC	O.K. Zack, last one on this.
Zack	Body books.
PC	What do body books tell us?

Zack	About your bones inside – about inside of you.
Comment	*Zack makes a claim to knowledge on the basis of authority – in this case, the authority of the textbook. For a discussion of the concept of 'authority' and children's views of it, see Chapter 6.*
PC	This class is working very well this morning – thinking very hard. Ryan?
Ryan	Our bones are in the same place.
PC	Yes, our bones tend to be in the same place, don't they? Jason?
Jason	Sometimes bones can be broken and they might not be in the same place.
Comment	*Jason offers a counter-example. The ability to do so is enhanced by learning the skills of argument (see Chapter 6).*
PC	No, they might not. And what happens to us if our bones are broken? Shauni?
Shauni	If your bone is broken on your leg, you can't walk. If your bone breaks on your arm, you can't carry things with that arm.
PC	You can't. So what does the doctor do for us when we have a broken bone? Let's say we have a broken arm. Jason?
Jason	Gives us an X-ray.
PC	Gives us an X-ray first. What does he or she do then?
Michaela	Have an operation. An X-ray.
PC	Sometimes we might need an operation if it is a very bad break.
Nathan	They move your bone in the right place.
PC	Excellent, say that again, Nathan.
Nathan	They move your bone in the right place with some gloves.
PC	With some…
Nathan	Special gloves.
PC	O.K. Jonathan?
Jonathan	Sometimes, if you broke your arm, you have to put your arm there and they bandage it. There's like a little rope and you can hold your hand by there. To pull your muscle; to go like that.
PC	And when our arms are better?
Jonathan	You can take it off.
PC	And then the arm is just like…
Jonathan	Normal.
PC	And it has gone back to the…
Jonathan	Right place.
PC	Now where did I get to? Scott and Shani. Tell me one thing, Scott, that's different between you and Shani.
Scott	We haven't got the same jumpers.

PC	You haven't got the same jumpers. And Shani, tell me one thing that is the same.
Shauni	We've got the same ears.
PC	You've got the same ears – excellent. Zack and Jason. Jason, tell me one thing that is the same between you and Zack.
Jason	Our shoes are the same – black.
PC	Zack, tell me one thing that's different.
Zack	Our trousers are different.
PC	How are they different?
Zack	Because mine are jeans and his are trousers.
PC	Excellent. Last two – Ryan and Shauni. Shauni, tell me one thing that's the same between you and Ryan.
Shauni	Lips.
PC	Yes, you've got the same lips. And one thing that's different, Ryan?
Ryan	Our hair.
PC	How is your hair different?
Ryan	It's a different colour.
PC	… Now we are going to see a small clip from a *Sesame Street* video. And it's about children's faces. And what I'd like you to do is look very carefully and listen very carefully to what people are saying, and then I'm going to ask you some questions about what you see…
Comment	*The lesson moves on from a consideration of similarities and differences between pupils in a particular class, to those which are thought to exist between children in a broader international context. The class views a brief excerpt from* Sesame Street: We All Sing Together[1] *which focuses on a song about 'Faces':*

An eye over here and an eye over there,
A nose in the middle, on top some hair.
A mouth at the bottom and the ears in place,
Put them all together and you make a face.

Chorus: Faces! Faces!

Every face is different: some are big, some are small,
Different colours, shapes and sizes, can you count them all?

Chorus: Faces! Faces!

There are round ones, long ones, tall and wide,
You can see them from the front, you can see them from the side.

Chorus: Faces! Faces!

Faces look different, there's a lot they share,
I can show how I'm feeling, you can show you care.
I can tell when you're happy, I can see when you're sad,
You can show it when you're angry, yeah, really mad!

Chorus: Faces! Faces!

Black hair, blond hair, red and brown,
Curly or straight, wear it up or down.
Funny faces, silly faces, one, two, three,
Just look in the mirror, tell me what you see.

Chorus: Faces! Faces!

Blue eyes, brown eyes, grey and green,
I think I'm beginning to see what you mean.
Got a nose to smell with, we've got ears to hear,
The song we're singing should be pretty clear.
We're a lot alike, that's the place to begin,
And we're all wrapped up in different coloured skin.

Chorus: Faces! Faces!
                 Faces! Faces!
                 Faces! Faces!
                 Faces!

MB	Now can you tell me some of the things that were the same about those faces? Kaylee?
Kaylee	Two of them had a hat on.
MB	Some had hats on. Jonathan?
Jonathan	Some had the same colour skin and some had brown skin.
MB	Right, good boy. Michaela?
Michaela	Some had the same coloured hair.
MB	Some had the same coloured hair. Zack?
Zack	Some had the same kind of ears.
MB	Dakota?
Dakota	Some had the same colour eyes.
MB	Good girl. Shauni?
Shauni	They all had faces.
MB	They all had faces – that was the same about them all. Good girl. Nathan?
Nathan	Because there's Spanish people and there's American people, Australian and some in Wales, and English people.
MB	Yes. Alisha?

Alisha	Some people had short hair and some people had long hair.
MB	Shall we talk about what's different about the faces? Natasha?
Natasha	They all had different kinds of faces.
——	Some were round.
Nathan	He's got a different face.
Michaela	Some had dark faces and some had light faces.
Jonathan	Some had brown skin, some had our skin.
MB	What's your skin?
Jonathan	Peach.
MB	Your skin's a peach colour do you think? Jason?
Jason	Some faces were big, some faces were little.
Zack	Some had freckles and some didn't.
Nathan	Some people had delicate skin.
MB	Delicate skin. What is delicate skin?
Nathan	I forgot what it means now – I knew a minute ago.
MB	Perhaps you will remember a bit later. Does anybody else know what 'delicate' means? Amy?
Amy	You can hurt it easily – soft skin.
MB	Yes, soft skin – that is sometimes very delicate.
Jason	Smooth skin.
MB	Jonathan?
Jonathan	When Zack said 'People have freckles and some don't', I went like that [Jonathan puts his hands over his face] because I've got freckles.
MB	Right – anything else you can tell me that's different about the faces?… We've talked about what was 'the same' and we've talked about what was 'different'. What I want to know from you now, were there more things the same about the faces or were there more things that were different?
Zack	Different.
MB	There were more differences?
Dakota	The same.
MB	There were more things the same? Why do you think that there were more things the same, Dakota?
Dakota	Because their faces, they all had eyes the same. Some had green eyes but they were the same shape of the eyes and the same shape of the nose and mouth.
MB	Good girl. Jason?
Jason	Some were girls, some were boys.
MB	Some were girls, some were boys. Were there more boys than girls do you think?
Boys	More girls.
Girls	More boys.
MB	Michaela?
Michaela	There were more boys.

MB	And did you think there were more things that were different about the faces than the same?
Michaela	Different.
MB	Different? Does it matter that we are different?

Comment   *This is a crucial question in the context of international education.*

Chorus	No!
Nathan	If we were the same, no-one would know who we are.

Comment   *Nathan returns to the issue of personal identity. His argument to justify its importance is supported by a relevant reason.*

MB	If we were the same, no-one would know who we are.
Zack	It can matter because some people might be picking on other people if they've got freckles.

Comment   *Zack's argument involves an account of the possible consequences of perceived differences.*

MB	So do you think it matters that we are different?
Zack	Only a bit.
MB	Only a bit. And why does it matter a bit that we're different?
Zack	Because people might pick on people if they've got freckles.
MB	People might pick on you. Why might they pick on you if you've got freckles?
Zack	They might not have freckles.
MB	They might not have freckles. So why should they pick on you if you've got freckles?
Zack	Because they might be jealous.
MB	They might be jealous – right. Does it matter that we're different? That's my question. Gareth?
Gareth	If you're the same, they won't recognise you…
Jonathan	We are the same inside but not outside.
Dakota	We are still special to our mums.
MB	We are still special to our mums, Dakota said.
Dakota	And our dads…
Scott	Some children look like their mums.
PC	Now I have one last question I'd like to ask… Which do you think is more important, how you look or how you behave? Helen?

Comment   *In asking this question, my aim was for children to consider alternatives, to discuss their values (an important element of personal, social and moral education, which is the subject of the next chapter) and to arrive at considered judgements.*

Helen	How you behave.
PC	Why is how you behave more important, Helen?

Helen does not reply.

PC	I'll come back to you. Shauni, what do you think?
Shauni	If you behave badly, you'll turn out like a bad person and if you behave goodly, you'll turn out like a good person.
PC	That's excellent. Jonathan?
Jonathan	If you was naughty every day, you'd be really naughty. But if you look different, it doesn't matter; but if you are naughty every day, it does matter.
PC	Why does it matter?
Jonathan	Because if you're naughty every day, it's hard work for your mums and dad, and she just won't cope with it.
PC	Jason?
Jason	Your mum and dad will get fed up and they'll get angry.
PC	Zack?
Zack	Your mum and dad might send you to bed and you might be grounded.
PC	You might be grounded. Jonathan again?
Jonathan	Sometimes if you're naughty, your mum gives you a smack and you wouldn't like being smacked.
PC	No, you wouldn't. Dakota?
Dakota	If one of our mums was pregnant and if their tummies hurt very much, and if we were annoying them all the time, they would be mad and they wouldn't shout, they would just send us to bed.
PC	They would just send you to bed. Does anyone else want to say to me anything else about which is most important: how you look or how you behave?
Nathan	How you behave.
PC	Why, Nathan?
Nathan	Because if you're not well behaved, then your mums will be after you and there'll be mums nagging and it won't be very nice. And if the cop car's coming round, then your mum could get in jail for a couple of years – for about twenty-five years. And if you're naughty and you throw stones at cars, and there's an alarm on it and the police come and you're holding any, they'll take you in prison. And then, when you come back from the jail, then your mums might say that you're grounded or something and give you a smacking, and say 'Go to bed', because it's hard work for your mums and dads, your nans and aunties and *taids* [grandfathers]. So that's why you have to be well-behaved.

Comment   *Nathan's contribution indicates that young children are capable of sustaining an argument at some length, by offering several reasons in its support. This is an important aspect of the proposed model of argument which is outlined in Chapter 6.*

PC   Excellent, what a good boy. Now we'll have three more comments. Kaylee first.

Kaylee   If you've been naughty and you're mum gets fed up, she'll just smack you and send you to bed without any supper.

PC   O.K. Zack?

Zack   They're the same.

PC   What are the same?

Zack   What they're like. They are the same importance.

Nathan   No, it's about being behaved.

PC   What you look like and how you behave, do you think they are the same?

Zack nods.

PC   Why are they the same, Zack, because you said they are 'the same importance'. Why are they 'the same importance'?

Zack   Because if you're being naughty, your mum will give you a smack, and what you look like, if you're the same, no-one will be able to recognise you.

Comment   *Zack's comment demonstrates that he has listened attentively to the discussion and is able to summarise his argument in a concise manner.*

PC   Last one – Jason?

Jason   Your mum will send you to bed without any dinner.

PC   She will. Well, I can say one thing – we are going to stop now. Nobody is going to be sent to bed tonight because everybody today has been a word beginning with 'e'…

Chorus   Excellent.

PC   Excellent.

Comments on the dialogue

In concluding the chapter, I offer some brief comments. Firstly, I suggest that this dialogue offers ample evidence of young children's capacity to think, reason and argue in a competent (and often skilful) manner about a range of issues. Secondly, many authors have provided valuable guidance (often in the form of summary points) for teachers about how to facilitate and assess progress in discussions with their pupils. My own approach in this book is to offer extensive dialogues, punctuated with commentaries, so that practitioners can deepen their understanding of how such work might take place in practice by examining critically some examples of it from the infant classroom.

Finally, I return to the comment made by Matthews (1980, p. 14) in Chapter 1, concerning an anecdote offered by three-year-old Denis which, it is suggested, '… is perhaps pre-philosophical rather than philosophical. It doesn't really pose a philosophical problem, let alone attempt to solve one. But it does incorporate the kind of play with concepts that nurtures philosophy'. While agreeing with Matthews' view in this particular context, I do not feel that it is appropriate to refer to the comments made by young children, in dialogues such as the one discussed above, as 'pre-philosophical'. In support of this argument, I would only point out that while pupils in the early years of their education strive to develop an understanding of, for example, mathematics, it is not suggested that the subject and outcomes of their endeavours are either 'pre-mathematics' or 'pre-mathematical'. In this context, why should philosophical reasoning be regarded as any different to mathematical, scientific any other form of reasoning to which children are introduced? As no adequate rationale has been adduced to support this distinction, I suggest that 'Developing Philosophical Thinking in the Early Years Classroom' is entirely appropriate both as the title of this chapter and as an educational aim.

Note

1. The title of the videotape is *Sesame Street: Learning to Share and We All Sing Together* (Children's Television Workshop, 1998; distributed in the UK by Buena Vista Home Entertainment Ltd).

Chapter 5

Thinking Skills and Personal, Social and Moral Education

In the introduction to this book, I referred to the work of the former School Curriculum and Assessment Authority and to its view that 'the task of schools, in partnership with the home, is to furnish pupils with the knowledge and the ability to question and reason which will enable them to develop their own value system and to make responsible decisions on such matters' (SCAA 1995, p. 6; see also DeVries and Zan 1994). How might such an endeavour be accomplished in the classroom? The excellent work of the Citizenship Foundation in developing teaching materials for use in schools has already been noted in Chapters 2 and 3 (see also Rowe 1992, 1998). In what follows, I examine a programme for promoting personal, social and moral education which I developed with Maggie Bowen. I shall then explore a dialogue which took place with a class of five- to six-year-old pupils.

Issues in personal, social and moral education

The programme is entitled *Issues in Personal, Social and Moral Education*, and consists of four volumes: *Deadly Habits?*, *The Rights of the Child*, *Family Values*, and *What are Animals' Rights?* (Bowen and Costello 1996a, 1996b, 1997a, 1997b), together with a teachers' handbook (Bowen and Costello 1996c). *Issues* is intended primarily for use with pupils at Key Stage 2 and the aims of the series are to:

provide teachers with a resource to meet specific National Curriculum requirements;
increase pupils' knowledge and understanding of a range of topical issues in personal, social and moral education;
enable teachers to develop pupils' value systems;
develop pupils' skills in speaking, listening, reading and writing;
promote pupils' reasoning and argument skills;
encourage pupils to work cooperatively and to respect one another's viewpoints;
encourage independent thinking and decision making
(Bowen and Costello 1996c, p. 1).

Each book aims to develop argumentative skills beyond the requirements of the National Curriculum. Pupils are introduced to a range of information related to a particular theme and incorporating a selection of moral and values issues which will help them to develop self-awareness, decision-making skills and the ability to think and behave in a reasonable and responsible manner. Topics in the series are divided into three sections. In the first, pupils are given a collection of relevant data outlining key issues for discussion. These have been taken from a variety of sources and provide a broad perspective against which the topic in question may be viewed. The second section contains a selection of pictorial representations each with a number of discussion points. Finally, in section three, a story featuring several important themes provides a basis for discussion and argument. This approach has been adopted to enable a variety of teaching methodologies to be used in the classroom and to cater for pupils' individual learning needs (Bowen and Costello 1996c).

Using a model which focuses on the processes of argument (see Chapter 6), the four volumes attempt both to introduce children to current issues in personal, social and moral education and to offer a structure by reference to which critical thinking skills may be taught, learned and assessed. As an example of the teaching materials which have been produced, I offer the following story which I wrote to focus attention on issues such as animal rights, fairness, respect for others, prejudice and discrimination (Bowen and Costello 1997b, pp. 10–12):

All the fun of the circus

Leo, the lion cub, was bored. He had been on holiday from lion school for two weeks and did not have anything to do. 'I'm tired of doing nothing,' he told his mother, 'can't we go out for the afternoon?' 'Not today, I'm afraid,' his mother the lioness replied, giving him her usual irritable look. 'I'm busy. I've got to do the hunting and then prepare the evening meal. I haven't seen your father all day – he's probably out somewhere sunning himself'. Leo stretched out on the ground. It was a very hot day and the sun beat down on him remorselessly. 'And don't get under my feet,' his mother growled, moving towards him with a purpose. 'If you want to do something useful, practise your roar. If you're going to be king of the jungle one day, you've got to learn to roar. Then, when you're walking about, all the other animals will know you're coming and they will stay out of your way. Also you need to practise walking. Never walk quickly. This might give others the impression you're nervous. Practice a slow walk with your head held high in the air. They should teach you those things at lion school – I don't know why we send you there'.

Leo got to his feet and walked away – slowly. He tried to roar but his throat was a little dry and he coughed instead. 'Hello, Leo, why are you coughing? Are you unwell?' Leo turned round. A huge lion filled the clearing. 'Hello, dad! I'm fine – where have you been?' 'Walking down by the river. I heard a new circus was in the area and I went to have a look. 'Can we go please, dad? Can we? I'm bored!' said Leo. 'Tell you what,' replied his father, 'let's ask your mother and we can all go together. It's much too nice a day to be hunting'. Leo's mother agreed to accompany them reluctantly. 'I wish *I* was on holiday', she said quietly to herself. But Leo knew that, secretly, his mother was looking forward to the trip.

After a pleasant stroll, the lion family arrived at the circus. There was a large crowd waiting to be admitted. Lots of Leo's friends were there with their parents. Leo wanted to go off to join them but his mother whispered: 'No, Leo, let them come over to us. Remember what I said this morning'. One by one, the other young animals walked over, their parents a few steps behind. 'Hello, Leo', said Paul and Percy the piglet twins. Leo nodded with his head as high in the air as he could manage. Roberto, the young rhinoceros, bounded over. 'Hi, Leo. This circus should be fun. Shall we go to the front of the queue?' Leo's father had already begun to walk towards the entrance. On seeing this, the other animals jumped back and allowed him to pass through the crowd. Leo watched how slowly he walked. 'It must be good to be the king', he thought to himself.

Once inside the large tent, Leo and his family found a comfortable spot right next to the ring. The rhinoceros family tried to follow but Leo's dad frowned at them. 'Better sit well back', Roberto's father said, 'we'll see more from here'. The circus animals were already in the ring but Leo was confused because he didn't recognise any of them. 'What sort of animals are these, dad?' he asked. 'Humans, of course'.

Looking out from the nearest cage, two male adults were throwing plastic balls to each other and catching them in their mouths. A sign attached to the bars said 'No feeding the humans'. 'That one's got a beard like you, dad!' shouted Leo. His father laughed. 'Yes, and they've been trained to roar like us as well. They're very clever really'. In the next cage, two young girls were performing gymnastic exercises on a wooden beam. One became distracted by the noise the audience was making and fell to the ground. 'Ha, ha, ha, ha', laughed Harriet the hyena, 'Did you see that? I'm really enjoying this!' 'Hee haw' bellowed Desmond, the young donkey, 'When's the show going to start?'

Suddenly, the lights were dimmed and two elephants trumpeted the entrance of the performing humans. A family of six people came into the ring on all fours. They were dressed in their best clothes and were being ridden by monkeys. 'Let's see who can go fastest!' screamed the ring master, a huge bear. The humans raced across the ring trying to be the first to reach some food at the other end. One of the adults won and grabbed his prize – a huge grapefruit – and began to eat it noisily. Leo watched carefully. After a while, he said to his father: 'I know that one day I'm going to take your place as king of the jungle but, if you don't mind me asking, isn't this cruel?' 'Of course not, Leo,' his father replied. 'As you can see, these humans are well looked after. They get enough to eat, we give them a place to live and all for doing a few tricks. In fact, we're actually doing them a favour because, if they lived in the wild, they wouldn't last for very long at all. I thought you would have learned this at lion school. Really, I don't know why we send you there!'

The following questions are suggested for discussion (Bowen and Costello 1997b, p. 12):

- What sort of things should Leo be taught at lion school?
- Why did Leo's mother not allow Leo to join his friends?
- Why did Leo not reply to Paul and Percy? Should he have done so?
- Why did Roberto suggest that Leo and he go to the front of the queue? Should they have done so?
- What do you think about the idea of a circus that only contains humans?
- Why does the sign say: 'No feeding the humans?'
- Should Harriet the hyena have laughed when one of the girls fell from the wooden beam? Could Harriet help laughing?
- Why were the six humans dressed in their best clothes?
- Why does Leo think the circus is cruel?
- Are the humans being well looked after as Leo's father suggests?
- Is performing in a circus preferable to living in the wild?

This personal, social and moral education programme may be adapted for use in the early years classroom. Stories such as the above, if read to pupils by the teacher (see Chapter 3 for a justification of this approach), are likely to provoke thoughtful discussion. Some of the above questions may require adaptation – I suggest the following as possibilities to initiate a dialogue:

- Have you ever been to a circus? What did you see there?
- Why does Leo want to visit the circus?
- Leo goes to lion school. What do you think he learns there?
- When Leo and his family arrive at the circus, his mother does not let him join his friends. Why do you think this is?
- Paul and Percy, the piglet twins, say 'Hello' to Leo. What does Leo say to them?
- Should Leo have replied to Paul and Percy? What should he have said?
- Roberto suggested that Leo and he should go to the front of the queue. Do you think they should do this?
- Why does Leo think the circus is cruel?

Stories such as the above are accompanied by drawings which enable young children to contextualise the narrative and so derive a deeper meaning from it than would be possible from words alone. A video presentation also enables a synthesis of language and visual imagery to take place, which is one reason why those who experience the scenarios featured in *Sesame Street* find them to be both interesting and intellectually stimulating. The following dialogue, with Class A, focuses on the theme 'Helping others and being helped by others'.

Developing children's moral thinking

MB	The story that we are going to have today, with Ernie and Bert in it, is all about helping – helping people who have got a problem. Can you tell me if you've ever helped anybody that has got a problem?
Comment	*The first part of the lesson focuses on instances where children have helped others who have a problem. This reference to past experience is an important aspect of personal, social and moral education.*
Jade	When they fall over.
MB	Did you? What did you do?
Jade	I took them to the teacher.
MB	And what did she say?
Jade	Said take them and wash their knee.
MB	And did you do that?
Jade	Yes.
MB	Good girl. [Bethan], what did you do to help somebody with a problem?
Bethan	They fell over and I helped them up and I told the teacher and they told me to… and I washed it for them.
MB	The same as your friend really, wasn't it?
Chloe	When a girl falled over…
MB	Oh! Everyone is falling over in this school, aren't they?
Chloe	And I told the teacher and she said: 'Did you see it?' and I said 'Yes'. And she said: 'Take her in and wash her head'.
MB	Wash her head. Oh this was a poorly head this time, not a knee. Have we got anybody else who's helped somebody who hasn't fallen over… helped someone in a different way?
Kelly	My mum was sitting on the chair yesterday and she fell off, and I helped her get up and the chair broke.
MB	Oh, dear me!
Kelly	And she's got a baby in her tummy as well.
MB	Oh, dear me – so you did have to help.
Alex	My mum fell down the stairs and she hurt her knee, and I went to get a plaster from the cupboard and I put it on the knee where the cut was.
MB	Oh that was nice…
Haydn	I helped my friend – he tripped over on a brick.
MB	Did he? And what did you do to help?
Haydn	I went to my house and I got him a plaster and I told his mum.
Alex	I helped my cousin who fell over a brick and he cut his finger and I told my aunty.

MB   Has anybody ever asked *you* for help? Has anybody ever asked you to do anything to help them?

Comment   *The focus now shifts to experiences of being asked for help.*

Kelly   My mum asked me to help her tidy up.
MB   Did she? And what did you do when you were tidying up? What did you tidy up for her?
——   The bedroom.
Kelly   All the bedrooms.
MB   What about you? Do you want to tell me what you did?
Chloe   My mum told me to tidy my bedroom.
MB   Right and you did that. That was helping – helping mum. Well shall we watch the video now? Now I'm going to ask you some more questions after the video. So you must listen to the video very very carefully, so that you can answer the questions…
PC   Now we're going to see a story – a very brief story about Ernie and Bert at the cinema. The story is about helping people and I'd like you to look at how Ernie and Bert behave towards each other and how helpful they are. After you've watched the story, we'll ask you some questions…

Comment   *Now the lesson moves on to consider the idea of 'helping others and being helped by others' in the context of an excerpt from* Sesame Street: The Best of Ernie and Bert.[1] *The scenario concerns a visit by Ernie and Bert to the cinema and is prefaced by a conversation between Gina and Big Bird:*

Gina: Hi, I'm baby-sitting Ernie's little cousin, Ernestine, and Big Bird's helping me.
Big Bird: Yeah.
Gina: And right here I have Ernestine's favourite book, do you see?
Big Bird: Uh huh.
Gina: Do you know why it's Ernestine's favourite book, Big Bird?
Big Bird: Gee, I give up.
Gina: Because Ernie and Bert are inside this book.
Big Bird: Ernie and Bert are inside this book? Ha ha! I don't think they'd fit! Well Bert maybe – he's pretty skinny.
Gina: No really, they are – look.
Big Bird: Oh it's a *picture* of Ernie and Bert. Gee, I remember when Olivia took that picture one day – Ernie and Bert were at the movies.

Ernie and Bert at the Cinema

Ernie:	It's a good movie isn't it, Bert?
Bert:	Huh?… Huh?
Ernie:	It's a good movie.
Bert:	Oh yeah, yeah.
Lady:	Excuse me, please. Excuse me. Oh I'm sorry. Excuse me.

A lady, who is wearing a very tall hat, sits in the seat immediately in front of Ernie.

Ernie:	Hey, Bert, a lady just came in and sat down in front of me with a big, tall hat. Now I can't see the movie. What do I do?
Bert:	Ah, I don't know. Figure it out yourself, Ernie; I'm trying to watch the movie. Shh, shh, shh.
Ernie:	I see… what'll I do? Hmm…

Ernie has an idea.

Ernie:	I know what. Bert, Bert, hey Bert – I'm going to change seats with you, Bert.

Ernie tries to swap seats with Bert.

Bert:	What are you doing? No, you're not, Ernie.
Ernie:	You can see and…
Bert:	I'm watching the movie.
Crowd:	Shh!
Bert:	I'm sorry [to the audience]. Come on, Ernie!

Bert prevents Ernie from swapping seats with him.

Ernie:	O.K., I can't see. Guess I'll have to think of something else. Hmm… let's see. Bert can see because he's sitting on a seat where he can see. Hmm…

Ernie has an idea.

Ernie:	I know what – I'll sit on Bert's lap.

Ernie tries to sit on Bert's lap.

Bert:	What are you doing, Ernie?
Ernie:	I'm sitting on your lap, Bert.
Bert:	Ernie, get off my lap! Come on, go on. Get off.

Bert pushes Ernie off his lap.

Crowd:	Shh!
Bert:	I'm sorry [to the audience]. Come on, get off! Now sit down and be quiet!
Ernie:	But how am I going to see the movie, Bert? I can't think of anything, Bert.
Bert:	Look Ernie, what is the trouble?
Ernie:	I can't see the movie, Bert. What'll I do?
Bert:	Just ask the lady nicely: 'Please lady, will you please take off your hat so I can see?' Now leave me alone so I can watch the movie.
Ernie:	O.K. Bert... Excuse me, miss? Lady? Would you mind taking off your hat so I can see the movie?
Lady:	Oh not at all, I'm sorry.
Ernie:	That's very nice of you.

The lady takes off her hat and places it on the seat immediately in front of Bert. Now he is unable to see the movie.

Lady:	Is that better?
Ernie:	That's fine. Thank you very much... Thank you too, Bert.

Bert tries to see the movie by moving his head around the hat and then sighs deeply.

PC	Now I am going to ask you some questions about this story. Before I do, who could tell me some things that have been happening in that story?
Lucas	Bert couldn't see because of that lady's hat.
PC	He couldn't see because that lady's hat...
Lucas	Because she was wearing it and then she took it off and she put it up.
PC	O.K., that's a good start.
Kelly	Ernie couldn't see. The lady took her hat off and then Bert couldn't see.
PC	O.K., so in the end, Bert, who started off by being able to see the film, wasn't able to see the film. Anything else that you noticed about that film?
Alex	When that big yellow bird said they were in the book, then when he saw it, he said: 'Oh, it's only a picture'.
Comment	*This aspect of the video excerpt raises philosophical issues involving concepts such as 'the person' and 'perception'. For a discussion of photographic representation in each context, see Abel (1976).*
PC	Yes, now let's start with that one, because the woman who introduces the story is called Gina. And Gina shows Big Bird a book

	and says this is Ernestine's favourite book. Why was it Ernestine's favourite book, I wonder?
Jade	Because it had him inside it.
PC	Because it...
Jade	Had him inside it.
PC	Because it had who inside it?
Jade	Ernie and Bert.
PC	O.K., because Ernie and Bert were inside the book. Now what do you think about that? Is it possible for Ernie and Bert to be inside a book? Because what does Big Bird say when Gina says that Ernie and Bert are in the book?
Amy	They're too big for it.
PC	They're too big for it. So how come Ernie and Bert are in the book?
Jodie	Because it's a photo of them.
PC	And is that the same thing?
Chorus	No.
Matthew	It could be a bigger picture.
PC	So is it possible for you to be inside a book?
Matthew	No.
PC	Unless it's a...
Chorus	Picture.
PC	Or a...
Chorus	Photo.
PC	Now let's have a think about the lady with the big hat – the big, tall hat. What do we think about her?
Jodie	She walked past the children and she said: 'Please can I sit here?'
PC	Yes. She was very polite when she came in wasn't she, because she said – what were the first words we heard her say?
Lucas	'Excuse me please... can I sit... can I get past?'
PC	She was probably going to say all of that but she just had time to say 'Excuse me, please', which is what we all say when we are being polite. And then she sits in front of Ernie, wearing this big hat. Now, what do we think about that? Should people come to the cinema wearing big, tall hats?
Chorus	No.
PC	Why not?
Comment	*In personal, social and moral education lessons (as in philosophical discussions generally), it is important for children to give reasons to support their views or arguments.*
Kelly	Because the other people can't see.
PC	Because other people can't see. So Ernie has got a problem, hasn't he? Now when we started this session, Maggie was talking about

	ways in which we could help other people. And one way in which we can help other people is when they tell us that they have got a problem. When they've got a problem, we can think to ourselves: 'Now, how can we help that person to solve this problem?' So let's think about Ernie's problem. Ernie's got a problem because he can't see… Ernie can't see, so what does he say to Bert?
Amy	'Please can we change seats?'
PC	Even before he says 'Please can we change seats?', he asks Bert a question… What is the first question he asks Bert?
—	'I'm trying to sit on your lap'.
PC	Even before 'trying to sit on your lap'.
Kelly	'What shall I do?'
PC	Excellent! That is exactly what he says. He says he's got a problem, he can't see the film, and says to Bert: 'What should I do?' What does Bert reply?
Lee	Go and ask the lady to take her hat off nicely.
PC	In the end, Bert says that, but he doesn't start off by saying that, does he? What is the first thing he says? Because what I am trying to find out now is: is Bert being very helpful to Ernie? What is the first thing Bert says to Ernie?
Jade	Can we swap seats?
PC	No, Bert doesn't say that because Bert has a good seat and Bert can see the film. What does he say?
Kelly	It's a lovely movie.
PC	Yes, right at the start they say about it being a lovely movie. Can anybody tell me what Bert says when Ernie asks: 'What should I do?'

Comment	*In asking the questions which follow, my aim was for pupils to discuss the nature of Bert's behaviour and to suggest alternatives to it.*
Jade	'I'm trying to see the movie'.
PC	Yes absolutely, that's what he says. He says actually: 'Figure it out yourself, I'm trying to see the movie'. Now what do we think about that? Is that being helpful?
Chorus	No.
PC	Not really, is it? What might Bert have said when Ernie asks him: 'What should I do?' What might Bert have said there instead of 'Figure it out yourself, I'm trying to watch the movie'?
Kelly	Tell him what to do.
PC	So what could he have told him to do? What could Ernie have done?
Haydn	Asked the woman to move to another seat.
PC	O.K. and that's what happened in the end but Bert…
Jade	But then the other person couldn't see then.

Comment	*Jade indicates that this course of action, while enabling Ernie to see the film, does not solve the problem in its entirety, as success is achieved by depriving someone else of the opportunity to view it.*
PC	No, and we are going to discuss that, because that is another problem isn't it? Now, Ernie has still got a problem because he can't see. Bert isn't helping him, so he decides that he's going to swap seats. And he doesn't really ask Bert does he?
——	He just moves him out of the way.
PC	He just tries to swap without asking. What do we think about that?
Haydn	It's not polite.
PC	It's not polite. So what should Ernie have done, instead of just trying to swap seats?
Jodie	He could have asked him.
PC	He could have said what?
Amy	'Please may I change seats?'
PC	That's a lovely way of saying it: 'Please may I change seats?', or 'Please may I...'
Chorus	'Swap'.
PC	'Swap seats'. O.K. Now, what happens when Ernie tries to sit on Bert's seat? What does Bert do?
Haydn	He pushes him off.
PC	He pushes him off and he says: 'I am trying to watch this film'. So now Ernie thinks again. Ernie thinks: 'I've got a problem; what am I going to do?' And then what does Ernie decide to do? Not swap seats, he tries to do something different...
Comment	*Here my aim was to emphasise the connection between thinking and action, as it is important for children to develop an understanding of this relationship at an early age. Personal, social and moral education is concerned not just with what children think, but in developing those dispositions which, on the basis of reasoned reflection, lead to appropriate action (see McGuiness 1995).*
Amy	He tried to sit on his lap.
PC	That's the next thing that happens. What do we think about that? Because it solves the problem, doesn't it? If Ernie can get to sit on Bert's lap, he is going to be able to see the film.
Jade	But when he sits on his lap, then Bert couldn't see.
PC	Bert's not going to be able to see – now is that fair?
Comment	*In the dialogue which I outline in Chapter 4, the notion of 'fairness' is raised by children themselves. Here, I refer to it directly. This is in keeping with my view that, while classroom discussions should focus*

substantially on pupils' own comments, the role of the teacher in initiating, developing and guiding dialogues should not be underestimated. I shall return to this point in Chapter 7.

Chorus	No.
PC	So instead of Ernie trying to sit on Bert's lap, what could he have done instead?
Jessica	He could have told the lady to take her hat off.
PC	That would have been a good way to solve that problem, wouldn't it? He could have asked the lady, but he didn't do that – he tried to sit on Bert's lap and Bert pushes him off. Now Bert's getting a little bit fed up, because he's missing the film. So in the end, he says to Ernie: 'Look, what's the trouble here? What's your problem?' and Ernie explains his problem. He says: 'I can't see the film. What should I do?' So what does Bert advise Ernie to do, finally?
Bethan	Ask the lady to take her hat off.
PC	Yes, he said: 'Why don't you ask the lady nicely?' – because we always ask people to do things nicely by saying 'Please' – 'Why don't you ask the lady to take her hat off?' So what does Ernie then do?
Michael	He asks the lady to take her hat off.
PC	How does he say it? How does he ask?
Michael	'Please can you take your hat off? I can't see'.
PC	And what does the lady say?
Michael	'Of course'.
PC	'Of course', and takes the hat off. And then Ernie says…
—	'Thank you'.
PC	He does. He says: 'That was very good of you'; 'That was very kind of you'.
Jade	And then the lady puts her hat on the chair and then Bert can't see.
PC	Now we've got a real problem, haven't we, because now Ernie can see and he's happy; Bert can't see and he's…
Chorus	Sad.
PC	Now think about this. Is it fair that Bert now can't see the film?
Chorus	No.
PC	Well, what would you say to someone who said to you: 'Yes, it is fair, because when Ernie had a problem, Bert wasn't very quick to help him with this problem, so therefore it is fair now that Bert can't see'. What do you think about that argument?
Comment	*Two comments must be made here. Firstly, my aim was for children to consider whether, given Bert's lack of concern for Ernie's problem, an appeal to 'fairness' might properly be used to support the lady's actions in preventing Bert from seeing the film. Secondly, it is important for teachers to refer to the notion of 'argument' in*

attempting to improve pupils' skills in this area. This word, together with associated terms such as 'reason', 'proof' and 'evidence', will then become a natural part of children's vocabulary.

Lee	It wasn't very polite.

Comment	*As regards my first comment, Lee remains dissatisfied with the lady's behaviour.*

PC	No, it wasn't very polite. So now we've got a problem right at the end – another big problem… Ernie can see; Bert can't see. Ernie says 'Thank you' to the lady and he also says 'Thank you' to…
Chorus	Bert.
PC	Now at that point, I just turned the video off…
Jade	Ask the lady to put her hat on the chair at the other side of her.

Comment	*An excellent example of critical thinking. Jade correctly anticipates my question: 'How could we solve this problem so that both Ernie and Bert could see the film?'*

PC	Now you've done something very, very clever there, Jade… Who can tell me what she has done that has been very, very clever?
Leigh	Ask the lady to put the hat on the other side, so that they both could see.

Comment	*Leigh develops Jade's comment by adding 'so that they both could see'. In this way, he attempts to solve the problem in its entirety.*

PC	You're a star, Leigh. Now the other great thing that Jade did was she actually gave me the answer to my question, but she gave me the answer to it before I could ask it! Because what I was going to ask was: 'How are we going to solve this problem – Ernie can see but Bert can't?' And you said, Jade?
Jade	Ask the lady to put the hat on the other side of her.
PC	That's great. And then everybody can see. So when we are thinking about solving problems and thinking about helping people, what we are thinking about is: how can we solve this problem completely?
Joshua	She could've lied it down on some chairs.

Comment	*Joshua succeeds in solving the problem. I now attempt to ascertain whether pupils can think of other ways to do this.*

PC	She could have. Where else could she have put that hat, as you've mentioned that, which would have meant that we wouldn't have had a problem right at the start?

Chloe	Put it under a chair.
PC	She could have, because when we go to the cinema, we don't put our hats and coats, and ice-creams and fizzy drinks on the chair beside us, do we? Or on the chair in front, we put them often…
Chorus	Underneath the chair.
PC	I'd like to think now a little bit about how we could help each other and I'd like you to think about it like this… Who can tell me some ways today that we could be helpful to other people in this class?

Comment	*Here my aim was to relate the central theme of the video excerpt (the importance of helping people who have a problem) and the discussion arising from it to children's lives in school.*

Haydn	If they hurt themselves.
PC	If they hurt themselves, what could we do?
Haydn	We could tell the teacher.
PC	And what would the teacher do?
Haydn	Take them inside and wash…
PC	And wash their…
Haydn	Hands.
PC	Or?
Haydn	Their knees.
PC	Or whatever. O.K., that's one good way we could help.
Chloe	If people didn't know where things are, you could tell them if you knew.
PC	Now, for example, I'm new to this classroom, aren't I, and I've not been to this school before. Now who could tell me where something important is in this classroom that I might need to use? For example, I'm very keen to use computers… If I wanted to use the computer in this classroom, who could… tell me where I could find one? Can anyone tell me where the computers are?
Chorus	By there!
PC	I can only see this blackboard.
Chorus	It's behind the blackboard. You can use that one or that one.
PC	Oh you've got two. Which of these is the best computer?
Chorus	That one!
PC	This one on the right.
——	But we haven't used it yet.
Haydn	I've got a computer that cost three hundred pounds.
PC	And do you know how to use your computer?
Haydn	Yes.
PC	Now Kelly said something important, because she said: 'We haven't had an opportunity to use it yet'. So therefore we're going to need

somebody's help in order to use that computer for the first time. Whose help are we going to need?

Comment	*This approach builds on Kelly's comments in order to take pupils' thinking forward and to reinforce the main topic of the lesson.*

Kelly   The teacher's.
PC   We're going to need the teacher's help. So very often in this life, we get help from other people, don't we? We get a lot of help from our teachers; therefore, it is important that *we* help people as best we can.

Comment   *The idea of moral reciprocity is being referred to here. This is best summed up in the 'Golden Rule': 'Do unto others as you would have them do unto you' (Matthew 7:12). See Bok (1995) and Appendix 2.*

Leigh   I've got a computer and it was a thousand pounds.
PC   That's a lot of money isn't it? O.K., now let's think about this. First of all, are there any other ways – we've mentioned some ways in which it is possible to help other people – can we think of any others? Ways in which we can help people in this class today? Jade?
Jade   We can be polite.
PC   Why is it important to be polite to people? Why is that a good idea?
Jessica   Because they will be your friend.
PC   They will be your friend if you're polite. Is that a good reason to be polite: because we want people to be our friends?

Comment   *Moral arguments may be distinguished from those which are motivated by self-interest. An essential aspect of personal, social and moral education is to introduce children to this distinction by appropriate questioning. Consequently, as they become older, pupils' responses in discussions such as this demonstrate an increased understanding of the division which exists between these two kinds of argument (see Costello 1993b).*

Haydn   It would be good manners.

Comment   *Haydn is already beginning to grasp this distinction.*

PC   It would be good manners – it would be a good thing in itself, wouldn't it?
Kelly   If you didn't say manners, they might have not said manners to you.

Comment   *Kelly offers an example of the 'Golden Rule'.*

PC	So that's important isn't it? If we want people to be polite to us, we should be polite to them. Any other ways that we could help people in this classroom today? Anyone do a very hard think for me and come up with another reason for being helpful or another way in which we could be helpful?
Kelly	If they don't know what to do, you could tell them.
PC	Yes, now can you give me an example of someone who doesn't know what to do and how you could help them? What if someone says to us, because we're doing some mathematics or we're doing some sums, later this morning, and someone says to us: 'I don't understand this question. Can you help?'
——	Yes.
PC	What should we do?
Jessica	You could tell the teacher.
PC	You could tell the teacher.
Matthew	You could help them.
PC	You could help them yourselves…
Michael	If you knew, you could tell them.
PC	Now if somebody has got a problem with their sums, is it better to try and help them or is it better to give them the answer?

Comment   *Here I was attempting to test Kelly's comment that 'If they don't know what to do, you could tell them'. To what extent are pupils prepared to accept this view?*

——	Give them the answer.
PC	Why is it better to give them the answer?
Haydn	Because it's very polite.
PC	Do you help them…
Chorus	No.
PC	If you give them the answer…
Kelly	Yes, but we are not allowed to do it in this school…
——	It's cheating…
PC	What do we mean by 'cheating'?

Comment   *The clarification of terms is, as I have suggested previously, an important aspect of philosophical thinking. It is also central to the discussions which take place in personal, social and moral education.*

——	They've got to figure it out their selves.
PC	O.K., so what we might think about is: we might help them, mightn't we? We might explain to them how to do the sum. But if we give them the answer, that isn't actually helping them to learn how to do those sums themselves. They just simply write the answer down.

O.K., that's very good thinking. Now, this is the last question I'm going to ask. We've talked a little bit about how we might help other people in this classroom. Now what I'd like to discuss with you is: let's think of ways people might help *us*. Can we think of any ways that *we* might need some help in this classroom today?

Comment	*The last phase of the lesson considers contexts in which children might themselves be the recipients of help from others.*

Kelly	Tell them where things are.
PC	Tell people where things are. Any other ideas?
Jessica	If they were new, you could hold their hand and show them where the books are.
PC	You could do. It's always important, isn't it, when we've got somebody in the class who is new to the school… Have we all had some experience of that, where new children come to the school?
Chorus	Joshua.
PC	Joshua, when did you come to this school?
Joshua	I've forgotten…. About three months.
PC	So how did we help Joshua when he first came to this school?
Alex	Tell him where everything was.
PC	And he had to get used to some new things. What was different, Joshua, about this school, compared to the last school you were in?
Joshua	Maths.
PC	How was Maths different?
Joshua	[inaudible]
Kelly	He didn't do 'Mousematics'.
PC	Very often when children change schools, they've got a different mathematics programme, so it's important to help them with their new programme.

Concluding comments

Teaching thinking skills in schools is about bringing children to an understanding that they have the ability to advance ideas, views and arguments, in ways and in contexts which are frequently not exploited by the traditional curriculum. When we teach moral reasoning, we do more than expose pupils to bodies of knowledge (although, in my view, we should certainly aim to achieve this too); we also introduce them to the idea that the giving of reasons for beliefs, actions and ways of life is of crucial importance.

Note
1. The title of the videotape is *Sesame Street: Learning About Numbers and The Best of Ernie and Bert* (Children's Television Workshop, 1997; distributed in the UK by Buena Vista Home Entertainment Ltd).

Chapter 6

Teaching Young Children the Skills of Argument

Learning to argue is one of the central objectives of education. Whether it be engaging in a debate, participating in a group discussion, or writing an essay, children's ability to employ argument and to anticipate and evaluate the arguments of others is an important measure of achievement (Costello and Mitchell 1995b). In this chapter, I examine the teaching and learning of argument with particular reference to early childhood education. Having offered an account of a research project which aimed to improve the quality of children's argument, I discuss a dialogue which took place with a class of Year Two pupils as part of that project.

The theory and practice of argument

For some years, a debate has been taking place about the theory and practice of argument in education. Many contributors to it have examined problems associated with the latter. For example, Dixon and Stratta (1982, p. 42) suggest that:

It's time that we English teachers asked ourselves what we hope pupils will learn from the activity. Is it going to be a debating skill, an ability to hold your ground, come what may? Or is the emphasis rather on thinking – on reasoning to discover what it is you think and feel about such an issue, and to present a considered, personal viewpoint?

Dixon and Stratta argue that teachers of English are so uncertain about what they are attempting to achieve that they either ignore the teaching of argument or suggest that such teaching is not properly the province of the English lesson. In suggesting that change is required both in terms of classroom practice and methods of assessment, they conclude:

...for really searching Argument, examiners will need to turn to course work and new forms of questions, where pupils have time to discover, clarify and have second thoughts about what they do think and feel, and the grounds for their beliefs (or recommendations) (pp. 53–54).

Similarly, other authors refer to problems such as children's inability to write arguments (Freedman and Pringle 1984), while Clarke (1984, 1994) refers to the reading of material containing argumentative content in schools as 'an area of neglect'.

Improving the quality of children's argument

Given the difficulties cited above, it became evident to many practitioners in schools, colleges and universities that there was a need to build on the insights developed in earlier work (see, for example, Buchmann 1988; Andrews 1989; Berrill 1990; Wilkinson 1990; Clarke and Sinker 1992; Weston 1992; Oléron 1993) and to conduct further research into both the theory and practice of argument. To this end, a project was undertaken by researchers at the University of Hull entitled 'Improving the Quality of Argument, 5–16'. Directed by Richard Andrews and myself and funded by the Esmée Fairbairn Charitable Trust, it took place over two years and involved the participation of twenty primary and secondary schools. Our final report (Andrews *et al.* 1993), examines some of the theoretical issues underpinning the research and contains accounts provided by teachers who participated in it, together with numerous examples of children's work and an independent evaluation of the project.

We offer the following stipulative definition of 'argument', suggesting that it is:

a process of argumentation, a connected series of statements intended to establish a position (whether in speech or in writing), sometimes taking the form of an interchange in discussion or debate, and usually presenting itself as a sequence or chain of reasoning (Andrews *et al.* 1993, p. 16).

The main objectives for the research were to:

  identify existing practice in primary and secondary schools regarding the teaching and learning of argument;
  examine the relationship between spoken and written argument;
  explore the relationship between argument, cognitive development and thinking skills;
  identify problems in the teaching and learning of argument;
  devise materials, approaches and strategies to improve the quality of argument (p. 2).

The approach adopted in the project involved practitioner research (Webb 1990; Elliott 1991; Maykut and Morehouse 1994). Teachers formulated their own objectives, detailed plans and assessment procedures for gauging improvement in argument. This work was supported by the project's two directors whose task it was to record progress and, on occasion, to contribute to classroom activities. Primary school projects focused on themes such as: 'Bias in historical documents'; 'Ways of seeing the world'; 'Exploring forms of written argument in the junior school'; 'The prevention of school-based bullying'; and 'Argument: from the antagonistic to the collaborative'.

Following the completion of this project and another which focused on the teaching and learning of argument in sixth forms and higher education (Mitchell 1994), a dissemination of their findings took place at an international conference and two books were produced. The first, by Richard Andrews (1995), explores his own doctoral research in this field and some of the findings of the two projects. The second, edited by Sally Mitchell and myself, is a collection of papers on the theory and practice of argument produced by speakers at the above conference (Costello and Mitchell 1995b).

The Esmée Fairbairn project provided much evidence to support the central thesis of this chapter, namely that young children have both the enthusiasm and the ability to formulate and evaluate arguments, and to think critically about a range of issues. In order to illustrate my point, I offer the following dialogue which took place with a class of Year Two pupils as part of a project entitled 'Our Island'. Pupils were asked by their class teacher, Pamela Rose (PR) to imagine that they had been shipwrecked and to determine their priorities. Among the topics examined in the discussion are: whether there is a need to have a 'boss'; organising a group; the nature of good leadership; and obeying authority.

PR	Do you think that we need to have somebody who is in charge, or do you think that we could manage without that?
Paul	I don't think we should have somebody in charge 'cos they could be bossy. So I think we could manage without one.
Fiona	I agree with Stephen. If you have a boss, they always boss you around.
Roger	I don't think we should have a boss because if you're saying something and I thought 'Oh, it's not a good thing. I don't know why they're bossing us around'.
Fiona	I think we all should be a boss. We all could be in charge.
Mary	If you had one boss, you could have good ideas and other people could have good ideas.
Paul	If the boss didn't have a very good idea, the other people might have a better idea. So we don't need a boss anyway.
PR	Could I ask William to come in here because I don't think he agrees with this.
William	I think we should have not a boss but bosses. I think we should just have the boss of every group. The people who thought of it [the activity] should be the boss.
PR	Who would those people be?
William	Simon, Tony, Samantha and me.
PR	Do you think you'd be a good boss?
William	At home I am quite bossy.
PR	Do you remember when you were talking about organising your

	group? You said you would listen to what people had to say and then you would let them have a vote.
William	If somebody else had a good idea, I'd let us have another vote and then we'd get good ideas.
PR	What would you do if someone didn't agree with your good idea?
William	I'd just tell them that it was a good idea and then we'd have another idea.
Tim	I don't think that's really fair, because if they have ideas I don't see why they can't do their ideas.
William	I just want to say something. If somebody had an idea to make one big thing, then they would need help to make that big thing.
David	But it might not be a big thing, William, it might be a small thing. And I think having a boss would be a good idea, because they wouldn't know what to do, would they, without a boss?
Paul	I quite agree with the voting, because if you had good ideas and the boss didn't agree with them, you could have another vote, or else he'd just ignore them.
Rachel	I wouldn't like having to have a boss because they would be a bit bossy.
David	Bosses are meant to be bossy.
Rachel	I know they are meant to be bossy, but they might not be bossy, might they?
Fiona	I don't think it's a good idea because they might ask us to do something we can't do. We might hurt ourselves.
William	I've remembered what I was going to say. I didn't agree with David because if somebody's idea got the most votes, I'd try it out to see if it worked. And then if it didn't work, I'd tell them that it was a silly idea and I'd get another idea.
PR	I'd like to bring Richard in now because you didn't want to be in any of the groups did you, Richard? Do you think there should be somebody in charge?
Richard	I think there shouldn't be anybody in charge.
Samantha	If there was somebody in charge, the other people might get fed up.
PR	Would you like to be in charge?
Samantha	I don't think it would be fair on other people.
William	Samantha, I want to say something there. Even though your idea was quite good, I don't agree with what you've just said. Because when your group goes off, they won't be able to know what to do. They need to have someone to show them where to go and lead them.
Paul	Well I quite agree with Samantha, because if I was the boss of a team I wouldn't like to be organising because they would all get fed up.
PR	Would you get fed up if someone was telling you what they thought you ought to do?

Paul	Yes.
William	So, Paul, how come you're not getting fed up because you're in David's group and you've got a boss?

[Long silence]

William	Don't explain what you're saying, Paul, because I don't think you knew what you were saying and if you don't have a reason…
PR	Paul, why did you choose to go into David's group?
Paul	Because I thought it was an important thing to look for food and shelter for the night.
PR	Would you have gone into that group if you had thought that David was not a very good leader?
Paul	No.
PR	What makes David a good leader?
Paul	I know he can do things very well and he's never bossy. He never gets cross.
PR	Is that right, David? Are you that sort of person? Don't you ever get bossy?
David	Not all that often.
Tom	I think I'd like to have one person in charge and if people in the group had good ideas, we'd listen to those ideas and if they were sensible, we'd try them out.
William	Tom, your idea is just quite like mine, except he isn't voting. You're just choosing ideas there. So it's exactly the same as mine that idea. I'd pick the idea that got the most votes. And then the one with a few less. And then I'd keep going down until I'd find a good one that would work.
John	I'd go into Tom's group, because if I was going to say something, he would listen to it.
Robert	I'd go with Tom, because say if William said 'Robert, do something', he might listen but I'd go with Tom. He'll listen to what we'll say.
Glen	I'd go with Tom because William would always boss you about.
PR	Are you a bossy person, William?
William	No, I don't think so.
Several	Yes, he is!
Paul	I'd like to be with Tom because he's nice and kind to me.
Jane	I'd be with Tom 'cos he does nice things.
John	I think William would talk too much.
PR	People seem to think, William, that you are a bossy person. Are you bossy?
William	Yes, I'm bossy at home.
PR	What would you do if you had a good idea and your group wouldn't accept it?

William	All I'd do is ask them if they had a better idea. And then it doesn't matter – we'd just carry on with mine.
PR	If there was nobody in charge, how would you decide what to do?
Paul	We'd just try out the good ideas.
William	I don't think that's a good idea because if people had silly ideas, what would you do then? What if everybody didn't have good ideas? If everybody didn't agree with each other, what would you do then? What would you do without a boss? Suppose you didn't have one, all you'd be able to do is everybody would be arguing. Everybody would think they had better ideas than everybody else. They'd always be arguing.
—	I agree with you there.
Paul	There would be no-one to help you if you needed help.
William	That's why I think you should have bosses because then everybody else wouldn't be arguing.
David	William, I think your idea on voting was good.
William	I know. If you voted, then that person would get to try out their idea. It's only to help you decide who is going to try their idea first and try it out.
Paul	I don't agree with having a boss because I wouldn't like to be a boss. I'd just let everyone do their idea and then we'd see if they are any good.
William	Paul, I think it's better to let people help you if the job's quite big, otherwise people would be arguing.
Paul	What happens if it's a small thing?
William	If it was small, you could just go off and do it and see if it works or if it doesn't.
Paul	What I would do is I would see if another person could do it first, to see if it would work.
PR	William thinks you would argue. Do you think you would argue?
Several	No.
Stephen	You would and no wonder – they'd be bossing you around. Like William, like he was saying to his group and they didn't believe him, and they could say: 'William, we don't believe you'. Because if we was in groups, and there was a boss there, we shouldn't have a boss.
Jane	I don't think we would be arguing because we would be worrying about getting back to land.
Neil	I quite agree with you there.
William	I think I know what you're going to say. They can't boss the other groups around because the other bosses will keep them in control.
PR	Suppose your leader asked you to do something silly like swim home from the island. What would you do if you didn't agree with them?
Jane	I wouldn't go swimming because some people might not be able to swim without armbands. Some people might not be able to swim at all.

PR   Suppose I said 'Jane, you are going to swim for home whether you like it or not', what would you say then?

Jane   I'd say it was a bit too dangerous.

I would like to make a number of comments about this dialogue. In particular, I shall focus on children's views on the notion of 'authority'. This concept is an important one in the educational domain and has, over the years, been the subject of close scrutiny (Peters 1973; Kleinig 1982; Allen 1987; Mackenzie 1988). In an article which examines the relationship between authority, moral education and the National Curriculum (Costello 1993c), I suggest that teachers who are non-authoritarian in outlook offer an excellent opportunity to children to develop their abilities to think, to reason and to argue. By demonstrating a willingness to engage in the critical scrutiny of beliefs, teachers are encouraging a similar disposition in their pupils.

This is evident from the above discussion in which it is clear that participants demonstrate a high level of independent thinking. Paul, for example, suggests that some people might have better ideas than the boss and so the latter is not required. William argues that the originators of ideas should become bosses. This links the notion of authority to an individual's competence or ability (as seen in terms of his/her contribution to the success of the group). William's conception of the role of a boss is an intriguing one. Rather than seeing it as necessarily involving the imposition of authority on others, it is viewed by him as a means to facilitate democratic decision making by the group as a whole.

William's link between voting and the development of good ideas is supported by Paul as a device to ensure that the boss does not ignore the views of others and so behave in an authoritarian manner. Towards the end of the discussion, Pamela Rose asks Jane what she would do if her leader suggested that she should 'do something silly like swim home from the island'. Jane offers two reasons why she would not agree to this. When Pamela substitutes herself for the leader of the group and asks Jane how she would respond to being ordered to swim towards home, the substance of the response given remains unchanged.

In my view, two of the most significant contributions to the discussion are made by William. The first is offered in reply to Samantha who had argued that she would not like to be in charge because it would not 'be fair on other people'. In suggesting that her group 'won't be able to know what to do. They need to have someone to show them where to go and lead them', William articulates a view of authority which has been advanced by philosophers and others and which has achieved a good deal of plausibility because of its utility value. Later, in response to Paul, William expands his argument:

What if everybody didn't have good ideas? If everybody didn't agree with each other, what would you do then? What would you do without a boss? Suppose you didn't have one, all you'd be able to do is everybody would be arguing. Everybody would think they had better ideas than everybody else. They'd always be arguing.

Once again an articulate defence of authority, supported by relevant reasons, has been advanced.

An argument model

One focus of the Esmée Fairbairn project was on evidence of improvement in spoken and written argument. To this end, a tentative model was produced which outlined the main features of argument and which was helpful in enabling assessment of it to take place in schools. Our model contains ten stages. We suggest that there are two forms of argument which are pre-verbal in nature. The first is simply physical and 'is evidenced in struggles or fights to make a point, defend a position or assert a right' (Andrews *et al.* 1993, p. 50). The second type of pre-verbal argument involves ways of communicating such as crying. Neither of these forms is age-related – one might expect to see either in evidence at any time in an individual's life.

Moving beyond these two levels, we suggest that there is a stage where the child is able to offer an opinion or a statement using forms of expression such as 'I want', 'I like' or 'I think' etc. This is followed by being able to offer a statement or opinion supported by a single reason. At this stage, we are looking not only for an ability to provide such a reason; we are also beginning to analyse and to evaluate the validity or quality of the reason itself. At stage five, a child will be able to state an opinion or proposition and to support it with two or more reasons or with different kinds of 'proof'. The sixth level is one in which the child demonstrates an ability to accommodate contrary arguments within his/her own perspective and to use them to enhance that perspective. For example, someone might say: 'Although John believes that X is true because... I would argue...'; or 'I think Susan's argument is quite a good one, but it still isn't satisfactory because...'.

We believe that a proposed model of argument should incorporate some reference to an individual's ability to sustain an argument, at some length, either in writing or in speech. In our final report (Andrews *et al.* 1993, p. 51), it is suggested that:

> In dialogue or group discussion or debate, this will mean listening to others' arguments and reinforcing one's own position accordingly; in a speech or in written argument (which are, on the whole, more univocal) this will mean sustaining an argument by any of a number of different strategies (e.g. a variety of different kinds of 'proof', use of refutation, multiple propositions, use of logical consistency etc.).

Levels eight and nine in our model focus on a child's ability, on the one hand, to evaluate both sides of an argument and, on the other, to come to some sort of reasoned judgement on the basis of this evaluation. Finally, at level ten, a child will understand that no argument offered ever represents the 'final word' in a discussion or debate; at best such an argument may serve as a starting point for future deliberation.

Two brief comments about the model are required. Firstly, we do not see it as being, necessarily, a developmental model (at least not in the sense that individuals begin at stage one and work through subsequent levels either in a specific order, or at a certain speed). We note, for example, that children may demonstrate abilities which relate to two (or more) levels of performance at the same time. Secondly, the model is a product of a series of value judgements. For example, it is assumed that:

> a disinterested awareness of the operations of argumentation is the most 'advanced' level, and that the ability to maintain two or more sides of an argument at the same time and mediate between them is more 'developed' than being able to argue one side of an argument well (in order to make something happen/change things in the world). This very formulation is itself arguable (p. 52).

A complementary schema, based on the work of one of the participants in the project, John Adamson, was developed to enable teachers to assess children's work (pp.47–48):

Assessing Progress in Argument
Processes of Argument

The pupil is able to:
1. express a point clearly
2. take a point of view, express an opinion
3. make a personal value statement
4. express a preference
5. give an example
6. give several examples
7. give appropriate examples
8. make a comparison
9. draw a contrast
10. use an analogy
11. use supposition
12. use persuasive language
13. give a reason
14. give a variety of reasons
15. give appropriate reasons
16. quote evidence
17. weigh up evidence
18. refer to own experience to support arguments
19. appeal to authority (of various kinds)
20. stick to the point, be relevant
21. show a degree of logic in the development of the argument
22. repeat an argument in another form
23. take into account others' points of view

Specific to Oral Argument

24. listen and respond to others' points of view
25. sum up the progress of a discussion or argument
26. speak at length, linking several points together
27. avoid diversion
28. speak with authority, and without hectoring or aggression

Specific to Written Argument

29. vary the structure of written argument
30. write in various forms (e.g. letter, dialogue, essay)
31. use appropriate connectives (e.g. although, nevertheless, on the other hand)
32. introduce and conclude well (if necessary)
33. write in a lively, readable way
34. be sensitive to the purpose of the argument, and to the audience

From an examination of this schema, it will be evident that the teaching and learning of argument is central both to formal programmes for teaching thinking as well as to all academic subjects and disciplines. Whether the forum for teaching is a specific thinking skills course such as Lipman's 'Philosophy for Children' programme, Richard Paul's Critical Thinking programme or Edward de Bono's *CoRT Thinking Programme*, or a particular discipline such as history, science or philosophy, a fundamental pedagogical principle underlying such work is that children should be encouraged to reason and to argue well. If one advantage of the schema is that it may be used to traverse disciplinary and subject boundaries, then a second is, I suggest, that it is not age-specific. In other words, the criteria suggested are ones which, for example, apply to and have relevance for both early childhood education and higher education.

In order to illustrate ways argument may be taught and learned in different contexts, I offer two brief examples. The first refers to the idea of teaching philosophy to young children which I discussed in Chapter 3. Here the schema is useful because it draws our attention to certain procedural considerations with which children should be acquainted in order to enable them to reason and to argue *as activities in themselves*. For example, when participating in a philosophical conversation or dialogue, children should be able to listen and respond to others' points of view, express a point clearly, give reasons, make comparisons and so on. In addition, the schema is important because it helps teachers and pupils to focus on a particular kind of argument (in this case, philosophical). So, for example, encouraging a child to show a degree of logic in the development of an argument, to give appropriate reasons, or to evaluate evidence may have a meaning in the context of philosophy which differs (sometimes quite markedly) from paradigms evident in history, science, theology etc.

I also use the argument schema as part of an in-service Master's degree module entitled 'Thinking, Reasoning and Argument in Education', to illustrate those processes of argument that teachers should seek to promote and enhance as part of a thinking skills course for children. This module explores various thinking skills programmes and focuses on key issues such as 'Encouraging Classroom Talk' (Howe 1992; Woods and Jeffrey 1996); 'Teaching, Questioning and Learning' (Morgan and Saxton 1991), and 'Facilitating Philosophical Discussions' (Whalley 1984; Costello 1989b; Fisher 1998).

My second example of a context in which it is important for argument to be learned and taught is taken from courses of teacher preparation offered in universities and colleges of higher education. Here my concern is to improve the quality of student teachers' arguments as a means to enable them to perform better as students (in relation to the theory of education) and, consequently, as beginning teachers (in relation to children, schooling and the educational process). My supposition is that if student teachers are encouraged to reflect seriously on the aims and purposes of education, on the arguments offered by educationalists and others, and on their own role as emergent teachers in the classroom, and if they develop their own reasoned (and perhaps competing) perspectives, then their teaching is likely to become increasingly concerned with open enquiry in which children will themselves be encouraged to think critically, to reason well and to argue skilfully and fairly. In order to facilitate these developments, the teacher educators' role is of the first importance. Students need to be acquainted with the theory and practice of argument, to understand its significance in their lives as teachers and, crucially, to be aware of its importance in developing the minds of those children in their care. I believe that the argument schema outlined above offers an excellent starting point to any discussion in which student teachers reflect both on their own academic work and on that of children.

In conclusion, I suggest that the teaching of thinking is inextricably linked with the teaching and learning of argument. An approach to teaching thinking which views argument as central is to be welcomed, not least because it should enable educators to focus on what specific programmes have in common rather than on what sets them apart.

Chapter 7

Early Childhood Education and the Preparation of Teachers

In this final chapter, I examine some issues concerning the initial and in-service training of teachers, with particular reference to developing young children's thinking skills. There is a sense in which all six preceding chapters have contributed, in their various ways, to such an examination. For example, in Chapter 1, I suggest that an essential aim of early childhood education is to promote effective thinking in pupils and I explore the problem of indoctrination in educational settings. In so doing, I argue that there is a need for teachers and students undertaking teacher education courses to become acquainted with the 'indoctrination debate' and to articulate their own perspectives in regard to it. This is, in effect, a call for a renewed emphasis on the role of educational theory in such courses.

Educational theory and practice

The relationship between theory and practice in education has been the subject of keen debate for a number years. For example, Anthony O'Hear has argued strongly against the view that the theoretical study of education is a necessary element in the preparation of teachers. In his *Who Teaches the Teachers?*, O'Hear suggests that 'what is vital in teaching is practical knowledge combined with emotional maturity and not theoretical knowledge at all' (1988, p. 26). In a subsequent article, O'Hear indicates the limited value which he attaches to the systematic study and evaluation of educational theories: 'the theoretical study of education, which I believe should be made available to those teachers who feel a need for it, might be more appropriately undertaken when one has gained some actual classroom experience' (1989, p. 23).

However, I would argue that one branch of educational theory, the philosophy of education, should be an integral part of courses of teacher preparation and, furthermore, that it should be judged by its effectiveness in offering practical help to teachers and students in schools (Walsh 1993; Kohli 1995). For example, in regard to the central themes of this book, to discuss the nature and purposes of 'indoctrination', 'education for citizenship', 'thinking skills', 'argument', and 'personal, social and moral education' is to engage (at least to some extent) in philosophical reflection.

The teacher as researcher

Accompanying a focus on educational theory in initial and in-service teacher education courses, there is a need to argue strongly for the notion of 'the teacher as researcher' and to ensure that both beginning teachers and their more experienced colleagues have an appropriate grounding in educational research methodology (Hopkins 1985; Bell 1987; Walker 1989; Denscombe 1998; Halsall 1998).[1] Most initial teacher education courses now require students in their final year to undertake a substantial project (often referred to as a 'dissertation' or 'thesis'). This piece of work offers those who undertake it an opportunity to engage in some small-scale classroom research (usually linked to the final school experience placement) and to explore related theoretical perspectives in some depth.

During the academic year 1998 to 1999, I supervised the theses of a number of students undertaking the BA Primary Education (with Qualified Teacher Status) degree. Of this group, four chose to focus their study on issues related to citizenship education and/or the teaching of thinking skills (Bralee 1999; Hewer 1999; Price 1999; Wiggan 1999); there was a particular emphasis on Key Stage 1 in two cases. Each student completed a research project and explored, in a thorough manner, the key issues associated with it. These theses demonstrate a sound understanding of the relationships between educational theory and practice and were undertaken with the active support of schools. Indeed, because of the recent interest which has been shown in the notion of educating pupils for responsible citizenship, students were seen as bringing important insights about the subject into their classrooms and so contributed to schools' curriculum development in this area.

Teaching thinking skills

As an introduction to philosophical issues in education and research methodology are both useful in encouraging teachers and students to focus on their practice in a critical, reflective way, I suggest that they are prerequisites for the teaching of thinking skills in schools. However, something else is also needed. In order to develop such skills, practitioners must acquaint themselves with the theory base that underpins individual educational programmes and also acquire an understanding of how they are taught in the classroom. One way to do this is to examine accounts of practice such as those presented in this book. Another approach would involve undertaking a course of study in relation to particular programmes (see Appendix 5).

As regards the former, I have included below two further dialogues, which took place with Class B1 and Class A respectively (see Appendices 3 and 4). Unlike those presented in Chapters 3 and 4, these dialogues are unannotated and are intended for discussion in both initial and in-service courses. The topics covered are the same as those featured in the two chapters and so reviewing the earlier discussions may be helpful as a first step. In analysing and adding comments to the transcripts, two questions may be useful to initiate an exchange of views: (1) What are the key themes of each dialogue? (2) What evidence is provided of children's abilities in regard to thinking, reasoning and argument? As regards the first of these, I offer some suggestions for dividing up the dialogue in Appendix 3.

Concluding comments

Throughout this book, I have referred to the *teaching* of thinking skills to children. Some colleagues in the field disagree with this perspective and suggest, with regard to philosophising for example, that this is not something which is *done* to pupils but rather is an activity in which they engage as equal partners. I suggest that such a view is only partly persuasive and indeed may have a detrimental effect on the successful introduction of philosophical thinking into schools. Certainly children should be regarded as equals in respect of the expression of their ideas and views. It is also true that we do them a disservice in suggesting, first of all, that we are keen to hear what they have to say and then letting them know (intentionally or otherwise) that we find their arguments to be silly, or unimportant, or too controversial to merit a full discussion.

However, while I have no wish to advance a view of children as the passive recipients of philosophical knowledge and beliefs, to assert that the relationship between teachers and their charges involves equality of status is, at best, misleading and, at worst, is likely to make the very idea of teaching philosophy in schools unappealing in many quarters. It should be noted here that to accord children such equality regarding the expression of their views, which is entirely desirable, does not imply a similar acknowledgement in the domain of teaching and learning. After all, it is presumed that teachers are people who have both a greater experience of life and a superior knowledge of the discipline. Given this, it is to be expected that they will accept responsibility for improving the quality of children's thinking and will do their best to ensure that appropriate learning takes place. This is not to say that teachers have nothing to learn from the arguments which their pupils advance – they certainly do – it is simply to acknowledge that society has given the former a role which, if it is denied or ignored, will lead to children's educational impoverishment.

Teaching philosophical reasoning constitutes an important addition to the school curriculum. To increase the likelihood of its successful introduction, we need to ensure that we do not claim more for it than it is likely to deliver. Such teaching does not attempt to replicate in children the forms of thinking usually associated with adulthood. Rather its broad aim is to foster, in a manner which is respectful of the child, those mental habits which are the foundation of successful living.

In summarising the central thesis of this book, I would argue that education is fundamentally concerned with the improvement of children's thinking. To this end, initial and in-service programmes should prepare teachers and students to undertake work the central aim of which is to promote critical thinking in the classroom. In addition to undertaking specific courses which focus on the development of pupils' logical, ethical and more general philosophical thinking, they should be encouraged to view all curriculum subjects as having the potential to enable pupils to: ask appropriate questions, seek evidence for assertions, evaluate evidence, offer reasons, take into account and respond to the views of others, advance arguments, and arrive at justified and justifiable conclusions. In seeking to enhance reasoned reflection in the adults of tomorrow, we must begin with the teachers of today.

In July, 1998, I was invited to present an address to teachers receiving the MA degree in Education at Viterbo College, Wisconsin. In my paper, which was entitled 'President John F. Kennedy and the Idea of an Educated Citizenry', I referred to a speech which the President made at San Diego College in June, 1963, in which he argued as follows: 'No country can possibly move ahead, no free society can possibly be sustained, without an educated citizenry'. Two questions arise from this statement: (1) What is it to have an educated citizenry? (2) What is essential to education for citizenship?

As regards the first question, I would argue that an educated citizen is someone who, in addition to having acquired knowledge, understanding and skill in a number of academic (and other) areas, is also disposed both to think critically, cogently and carefully about beliefs, attitudes and values, and to act in morally appropriate ways. In other words, there should be a direct relationship between thinking and behaving, between thinking well and behaving well. In response to the second question, I have suggested that any adequate programme of citizenship education should have at its core the explicit teaching of thinking skills.

Note
1. Recently, the nature and purposes of educational research have been the focus of critical scrutiny. See, for example, Tooley with Darby (1998); Hillage *et al.* (1998); and responses by Lomax (1998); Edwards (1998); Vulliamy (1998) and Atkinson (1998).

Appendix 1 – Short Stories which Introduce Philosophical Ideas

In order to introduce primary school pupils to philosophical ideas, I have written the following short stories.

Knowlittle, Knowless and Knownothing

There were once three children. They were called Knowlittle, Knowless and Knownothing. They lived in the kingdom of a very harsh king, King Extrawork. Now, King Extrawork was always imposing rules on his subjects. For example, if they wore black shoes in public, he would remind them of his rule: 'No wearing of black shoes in public,' and give them a heavy fine and some extra work. If they made bubbles with their chewing gum, he would remind them of his rule: 'No blowing bubbles with chewing gum,' and give them a heavy fine and extra work. So it went on: 'No reading books on Saturdays,' 'No riding bicycles on Wednesdays' and 'No "quarter-pounders" or milk shakes on any day of the week.'

At last Knowlittle, Knowless and Knownothing got fed up and decided to leave the Kingdom of King Extrawork and to live on their own completely without rules. 'We won't have any rules whatsoever,' they said, 'and so we will always be happy.' So they set up home together in the kingdom of King Eversonice, where there were no rules whatsoever. When they went to Eversonice Primary School, there were no rules to be obeyed: the children were not asked to study anything at all. Some children played marbles all week long. The teachers never gave tests, or extra work, and they never marked books. There were no exams because the children in the school said that they did not like them. In class discussions all the children shouted at once, and all the teachers smiled because there was no rule which said that children should be polite.

For a couple of days, Knowlittle, Knowless and Knownothing thought their school was a very good school but then they grew tired of playing marbles and longed for some real work to do. But, when they tried to tell the teacher this, they could not be heard because the other children were shouting. And all the time their teacher smiled.

One of the children in the class saw that Knowlittle had a big red apple, and he grabbed it and ate it in one mouthful. Knowlittle ran to his teacher and told him but the teacher said this was allowed because there was no rule forbidding stealing.

When it came to lunch time, several children pushed in front of Knowless in the dinner queue. Knowless complained to the dinner lady but she told him that there was no rule which said that pushing in was forbidden. And when it came to home time and the school bell rang, all the children rushed for the door without waiting to be told, and Knownothing was crushed in the battle which took place to get out.

'That's a terrible school,' said Knowlittle. 'Everyone does what they want.' 'I think the kingdom of King Eversonice isn't as good as we thought,' said Knowless. 'To have no rules is as bad as having bad rules. I wish there was a kingdom where the people had some good rules to live by, so that they could live together sensibly.' 'But where can we find such a place?' said Knownothing. 'I know one thing,' said Knowless, 'I'm not going back to that school. Let's leave this kingdom and look for somewhere new to live right away.' So they did. Do you think they found such a kingdom? What good rules would such a kingdom have?

The Snow Queendom

Having left the kingdom of King Eversonice, Knowlittle, Knowless and Knownothing began their search for a kingdom where people have some good rules by which to live. After many hours of travelling, they saw a sign which said: 'Snow Queendom: 1 mile.' 'I'm starving,' said Knownothing, disgruntled. 'If we hurry,' said Knowless, 'we will arrive at the Snow Queendom in time for tea, I think.' 'You're right!' exclaimed Knowlittle.

So they began walking more quickly and very soon they were approaching the city walls, which glistened in the distance. As Knowlittle, Knowless and Knownothing walked up to the entrance of the Snow Queendom, they noticed that its walls were all made of ice. Suddenly, enormous snow-flakes began to fall gently from the sky. One snow-flake landed directly on Knownothing's head and melted instantly, soaking him to the skin. He seemed totally confused and stood quite still. 'Quick, Knownothing, let's run before we all get wet!' said Knowlittle.

They ran through the gates, along the narrow streets, which were covered with ice, until they came to a large building which was made of snow. 'This looks like a hotel,' said Knowlittle. 'Perhaps we can get some tea here,' added Knowless. Knownothing touched an ice-cube on the front door and a ringing noise could be heard inside, which made him jump back in fright. 'I've never seen a door-bell made of ice before,' said Knowlittle.

After a few moments, a woman answered the door. 'Yes?' she asked, 'What can I do for you?' 'We have travelled a long way and we are very thirsty,' said Knowlittle. 'We were wondering whether you would be good enough to make us some hot tea. 'Hot tea?' said the woman in amazement. 'What a silly child! Don't you know that this is the Snow Queendom? We only serve cold drinks at this hotel!' 'Well, a cold drink is better than no drink at all,' said Knowless cautiously. 'Very well. Come inside,' said the woman. 'Be sure to close the door. The heat is making me shiver. If I'm not careful, I'll soon be getting a hot.' 'You mean a cold,' said Knowlittle. 'No, silly child,' said the woman. 'In the Snow Queendom we keep out the heat, otherwise we get a hot!'

Knowlittle, Knowless and Knownothing were all puzzled, and they followed the woman into a large living room which was so cold that icicles were hanging from the ceiling like chandeliers. Knownothing began to tremble uncontrollably. 'If you are warm, turn the icer on,' said the woman before disappearing through a large door. 'I think she must mean the heater,' said Knowless, thinking out loud, and he pushed the button at the front of what looked like an ordinary electric fire. However, instead of giving out heat, the bars of the icer turned white and sent out waves of freezing cold air. Knownothing shivered even more and began to look unhappy. Before he could complain, the woman reappeared with three iced-lollies. When he saw them, Knownothing smiled for a moment, before realizing again how cold he was. 'Swallow these,' she said 'they will soon cool you down.' 'Where we're from, we lick iced-lollies, or bite them; but they're too cold to swallow,' said Knowlittle. 'Nonsense!' exclaimed the woman in a loud voice. 'All children swallow iced-lollies. Everyone knows that!'

When they had finished the iced-lollies, the woman gave them iced-buns to eat and some cold coffee to drink. 'Allow me to introduce myself,' said the woman. 'My name is Miss Frost. Tell me, why have you come to the Snow Queendom?' 'We are looking for a place where there are some good rules to live by,' said Knowlittle cautiously. 'We have plenty of good rules here,' said Miss Frost. 'Our first rule is: "The Snow Queen is always right!"' 'Who is the Snow Queen?' asked Knownothing, still trying to eat one of the iced-buns. 'Why, our leader, of course,' said Miss Frost. 'She lives on top of a distant mountain in a castle made of the finest ice, well away from the heat. Although no one has ever seen her, we all know that she loves us and takes care of us.' 'If no one has ever seen her, how do you know she exists?' asked Knowlittle. 'Because she sends us the snow to keep us cold. Without the snow, we would have nothing with which to build our houses. She also sends ice so that we can build our roads. Roads are the very essence of civilization,' said Miss Frost in a firm voice. Knowless nodded nervously. 'How do you know it is the Snow Queen who sends the snow and ice?' asked Knowlittle. 'Because a friend of mine told me that each time the Snow Queen laughs, it snows. This is why we always do as the Snow Queen says, because this keeps her happy. When she is happy, she laughs. When she laughs, it snows, and so we are always cold. This reminds me of our second rule, which is: "To be happy, keep the cold in."' Knownothing shivered again. Knowlittle persisted: 'What proof does your friend have that it snows because the Snow Queen laughs?' he asked. 'You must go to a terrible school,' said Miss Frost sternly. 'Your teachers should have taught you that asking questions is a sign of stupidity! Surely you have heard of our third rule: "Ask no questions, the Snow Queen knows best."' 'That's news to me,' said Knowlittle, now shivering too. 'In that case, I'm not sure that we are going to be very happy here.'

Miss Frost Sets a Challenge

Miss Frost suggested that Knowlittle, Knowless and Knownothing might like to stay at her hotel for the night. 'I suppose your beds are made of ice,' said Knowlittle.

'Yes,' replied Miss Frost, 'and our pillows are made of the softest snow.' 'In that case,' said Knowless, 'I think we will continue on our journey. Would you be so kind as to give us directions to the nearest city?'

'Certainly,' said Miss Frost, 'but first you must answer three questions. If you do so, I shall give you the directions you require.' 'Very well,' answered the children together. 'I hope these questions involve thinking,' said Knownothing cheerfully. 'If they do, I know we will solve them easily.' 'I wouldn't be too sure about that,' said Miss Frost. 'I have asked these questions to many children who are older than you and no one has been able to answer all three successfully. I am sure that you will not succeed.' 'Just because no one has answered the questions until now, that doesn't mean that no one will ever answer them,' said Knowlittle firmly. 'Anyway, what are the questions?'

'I shall offer you three examples of reasoning,' said Miss Frost, 'and I shall ask you a question about each.' 'You must tell me whether the arguments are good or bad, sound or unsound, and why. The first involves two children, John and Sarah, who go to different schools. John says, "My school is better than yours." "Why is it better?" asks Sarah. "Because we are given homework to do." "Why are you given homework?" "Because I go to a better school." "What do you think of that argument?" asked Miss Frost. Knowlittle began to think about this carefully.

'What is the second piece of reasoning?' asked Knowless. 'I hope it is ice and easy!' Miss Frost smiled briefly. 'Imagine that you are playing out one evening. Suddenly, a boy, whom you have never seen before, comes up to one of your friends and pushes her roughly to the ground. Can you explain his action?' 'I'll think about this one,' said Knowless. 'That means that the third puzzle is mine!' said Knownothing. 'Tell me what it is.' 'Very well,' said Miss Frost. 'Ronald, a friend of yours, is going on a school trip. The cost of the trip is five pounds and today is the last day on which it can be paid. Ronald's mother gives him a five-pound note but he loses it on the way to school. At morning break, Ronald finds a five-pound note on the school yard. He puts it into his pocket. His friend Gerald comes up to him and says: "I've lost my five-pound note. If I don't find it, I won't be able to go on the school trip." What should Ronald do?'

Knowlittle, Knowless and Knownothing thought for a long time about the questions which they had been asked. Miss Frost gave them three ice-slates and ice-pens and they wrote out their thoughts with great speed. They returned the slates and pens to Miss Frost who examined them carefully. 'Why, you have surprised me,' she said eventually. 'You have all done very well. Usually, children just write what they think without bothering to give reasons for their opinions. But, you have offered arguments to support what you say, and now I shall give you directions to the nearest city. Now, let me see. If you turn left as you leave the Snow Queendom and walk for an hour, you will arrive in the Land of Youth. On the other hand, if you turn right as you leave the Snow Queendom and run for sixty minutes, you will arrive at the City of Books.' 'Which is the closest?' asked Knownothing looking puzzled. 'Why, the Land of Youth, of course,' said Knowlittle. 'Come on, let's go.' With this, Knowlittle, Knowless and Knownothing thanked Miss Frost for her hospitality and set off for the Land of Youth.

The Land of Youth

Knowlittle, Knowless and Knownothing began their journey in high spirits. They were looking forward to seeing the Land of Youth and they discussed what it might be like. 'One thing's for sure,' said Knowlittle, 'it must be warmer than the Snow Queendom!'

At that moment, the sun emerged from behind a large cloud and shone down on the three travellers. 'The sun must have heard you, Knowlittle,' said Knownothing cheerfully. 'Look, it's smiling at us.' 'Don't be silly,' said Knowless, 'the sun can't hear you because it doesn't have any ears. It can't smile at you either because it doesn't have a mouth.' Suddenly, the sun disappeared behind a very black cloud. The sky quickly grew dark and raindrops began to fall from the sky. 'Now look what you've done, Knowless!' said Knownothing in a vexed tone. 'You've upset the sun and now we're all going to get wet!' It began to rain more heavily and Knowlittle, Knowless and Knownothing had to shelter behind a large oak tree. 'I'm hungry,' said Knownothing, producing a large bag of sweets from his pocket. 'You're always hungry!' shouted Knowlittle. 'Eating too many sweets is bad for you,' said Knowless confidently. 'I know,' said Knownothing, 'but I can't help it. Each morning I tell myself that I am not going to eat any sweets today but I always do. I really want to stop but I just can't help myself.' Having said this, Knownothing swallowed all the sweets in the bag in one go. 'If you had really wanted to stop, you wouldn't have emptied the bag of sweets into your mouth,' said Knowlittle. 'Quite right!' exclaimed Knowless, 'you could have emptied it into our mouths instead. Really! Some people have no self-control!' 'What's the use trying if I know I'm not going to succeed?' said Knownothing. 'I may as well enjoy the sweets and save my energy.'

At this point, it stopped raining and the sun reappeared from behind the cloud. 'It seems that the sun has forgiven you, Knowless,' said Knownothing, 'come on, let's go.' The three children resumed their journey and soon arrived in the Land of Youth. A boy of about their own age greeted them. 'Welcome to the Land of Youth!' he said warmly, shaking hands with each of them in turn. 'My name is Falgan. What brings you here?' 'We are looking for a land where there are some good rules to live by,' said Knowlittle. 'In that case, you will like it here,' said Falgan. 'In this city there are no grown-ups to impose rules on us.' 'That's a good start,' said Knownothing happily. 'Perhaps our journey has come to an end at last!'

Appendix 2 – Classroom Dialogue 1

The following dialogue took place with a class of eight- to eleven-year-old children and is based on issues arising from my story 'The Land of Youth' (see Appendix 1).

PC	Knownothing says this… 'The sun must have heard you, Knowlittle, it's smiling at us.' What do we think about that statement?… Richard?
Richard	If you look at the sun, it makes your eyes go real funny. It makes you sneeze.
PC	Why does it make you sneeze?
Russell	It doesn't make you sneeze.
Richard	Brightness.
PC	[Does] brightness make you sneeze?
Richard	It makes me sneeze.
PC	Does it? What do you think about this statement, Michelle?
Michelle	You have no proof or evidence that the sun was smiling at him.
Comment	*In a previous session, the children had suggested two terms, 'proof' and 'evidence', which might be adduced in support of one's arguments. Their tendency to refer to both terms at once is a consequence of my having adopted this practice for mnemonic purposes.*
PC	Do you think the sun can smile at us?
Chorus	No.
Melanie	Yes.
PC	When does the sun smile at us, Melanie?
Melanie	When it's bright.
Russell	I used to think when the sun comes out, it was going to come down and play with me and when it goes back in a cloud it was going to go for his dinner, and then it came back out again and go for its tea and then go for its supper and then go to bed!
—	Laughter

PC	Well, I think the children in the story were having thoughts like that weren't they? What do you think, Timothy, about this idea of the sun smiling at us?
Timothy	When you look at it, really stare at it, it looks as though there's a big grin on its face.
Melanie	Yes it does.
PC	So, does the sun come out when it's happy…?
——	Matthew Parker shakes his head.
PC	No, Matthew?
Matthew P.	No… it's just amongst clouds what cover it up and then the clouds go.
PC	Doesn't it have something to do with whether or not the sun's happy?
Matthew P.	No, it's because of a cloud.
PC	So, what do you think about this statement… 'The sun must have heard you Knowlittle, it's smiling at us'?
Matthew P.	They have no proof or evidence that the sun come out just because they said something.

Comment   *Matthew spots the fallacy in a* post hoc, ergo propter hoc *argument.*[1]

PC	Let's say the sun had gone behind a cloud… and we said the words 'magic dust' and, all of a sudden, the sun came out and shone down on us again.
Matthew P.	That would just be… luck and timing.
PC	What if I said 'magic dust' and the sun came out, then it went in again, a little bit later, and I said 'magic dust' and the sun came out again. Wouldn't that give us the proof we require to say that what we said caused the sun to come out, Matthew?
Matthew P.	No, it would be the same - luck.
PC	What if I said it fifty times and each time the sun came out?

Comment   *I am attempting to ascertain whether the children will find the fallacy more plausible if there are a greater number of instances to consider. Russell remains sceptical.*

Russell	Still be luck.
PC	Why would it still be luck, Russell?
Russell	Because you've just got no proof or evidence that you are doing it, because you don't know, and if it's a real cloudy day, like it more or less is now, it'll probably just be luck.
PC	What about this statement… 'The sun can't hear you, it hasn't got any ears. The sun can't smile at you, it hasn't got a mouth.' What do you think about those statements?

Caroline	You have no proof or evidence that it hasn't got a mouth or ears.
PC	How would we get some proof about whether or not the sun has got ears and a mouth? Russell?
Russell	We can't.
PC	So does that mean we believe that the sun does have ears and it does have a mouth?
Chorus	No.
PC	Why do we not believe it then, if we can't prove that it doesn't?
Russell	We just can't, because we can't get to it. Well, we might be able to get to the sun, but we can't go on it.
PC	Well, why isn't that a reason for us saying: 'Well, the sun does have ears'?
Russell	You don't know whether it has.
PC	But you've just said to me you don't think the sun has ears... If I said to you: 'Well the sun does have a pair of ears and it does have a mouth', what would you say to that?
Russell	I'd think it would be stupid because you've got no proof or evidence that it has got ears or a mouth.
PC	So, what do you say to a person who says to you... 'The sun has two ears... and a mouth and you have no proof or evidence that it doesn't'?
Timothy	They have no proof or evidence that it does.
PC	So, are the two arguments as good as each other?
——	Some children say: 'No' and some say: 'Yes'.
PC	Why not, Russell?
Russell	Because it can't have ears or things, it can't.
PC	Why can't it?
Russell	Because it can't.
PC	Well now, watch this. I'm going to write on the board. I've said to Russell: 'Why can't the sun have ears?'...
Melanie	Oh, yes.
PC	... and Russell said... 'Because it can't.' [I write this on the board.] And I said to Russell: 'Why can't the sun have ears?' and Russell said: [I write 'Because it can't' on the board.] Have we met an argument like this one before?
Comment	*In a story called 'Miss Frost Sets a Challenge', Miss Frost offers Knowlittle, Knowless and Knownothing three samples of reasoning to evaluate. The first involves two children, John and Sarah, who go to different schools. John says: 'My school is better than yours.' 'Why is it better?' asks Sarah. 'Because we are given homework to do.' 'Why are you given homework?' 'Because I go to a better school.' See Appendix 1.*

Matthew P.	Yes, a round argument.
PC	No, it's not called a round argument... Melanie?
Melanie	A circular.
PC	A circular...
Melanie	Argument.
PC	Why do we call it a circular argument, Melanie?
Melanie	Because it just goes round and round and round.
Michelle	It's just repeating itself.
PC	What do we think about circular arguments? Are they good arguments, do you think?
Chorus	No.
PC	Why are they not good arguments, Michelle?
Michelle	Because they just carry on and carry on and they don't give you a good statement.
PC	They don't give you a good statement. They don't give you what?
Jayne	A good argument.
Caroline	Proof or evidence.
PC	Of what?
Caroline	Whether the sun has got two ears and a mouth.
PC	Excellent. Now let me ask you this... Knownothing says this: 'You've upset the sun and now we're all going to get wet!' What does he mean by that do you think?... Matthew P.?
Matthew P.	He's trying to say that they are all going to get wet, even though it wasn't him who said it.
PC	What do we think about that statement then?
Russell	Not very good because you can't upset the sun, because the sun can't hear you. It must be about sixty-eight million miles away.
PC	Ninety-three million miles away.
Russell	Has to have good ears, if it has got ears, to hear us!
——	Laughter
PC	Knowless says: 'Eating too many sweets is bad for you' and Knownothing says: 'I know, but I can't help it.' What do we think about that statement from Knownothing?
Russell	He's got no proof or evidence that he can't stop, because he might be able to stop, but he's got no proof or evidence that he can't.
PC	What did he do immediately after he had said this... Trudelle?
Trudelle	Went and swallowed the whole sweets.
PC	So, do you think he was trying very hard to stop... Melanie?
Melanie	No.
Russell	Yes.
PC	You do, Russell?
Melanie	He wasn't even trying.
Russell	Yes, because... if he swallows them, he won't taste them. So if he doesn't taste them, he'll get fed up of them and then he'll stop.

Comment	*Russell argues that swallowing the sweets is an exculpating circumstance, not an extra-inculpating one. This is something I had not considered when I wrote the story.*
PC	Do you think that was his intention when he swallowed the whole bag of sweets – not to taste them?
Chorus	No.
PC	Why do people usually eat things rather quickly, in that sort of way?
Caroline	Because they can't help it.
Samantha T.	Because they're greedy!
——	Laughter
Jon	It might be their dinner.
PC	Kelly?
Kelly	Could be hungry.
PC	Jayne?
Jayne	I eat my sweets fast, before my dad comes in, because he always pinches them all.
PC	Oh, your dad has one sweet tooth. A bit like me: I have a sweet set of teeth.
——	Afternoon break
PC	Immediately after Knownothing has emptied the bag of sweets into his mouth, Knowless says: 'Some people just have no self-control'… What do we mean by 'self-control'?… Michelle?
Michelle	It means that if you see something and you want it, your mind's telling you one thing to do and the rest of your body is telling you another thing to do.
Comment	*An excellent formulation of the dilemma facing a weak-willed person.[2]*
PC	And if you've got self-control, what happens?
Michelle	If you've got self-control, you listen to your mind and if you haven't got self-control, you just go and get that thing that you want.
PC	Can someone give me another expression for 'self-control'? Two words…
——	After several unsuccessful attempts, I say:
PC	Well, we'll have a game of 'Hangman' then, as we usually do.
Comment	*When the children are unable to give me the word or expression I am looking for, we play a game of 'Hangman'. This involves writing a dash on the board for each letter of the word or expression. I then give clues by inserting certain letters.*

PC	[I'll] give you the first letter of each word. Trudelle?
Trudelle	Will-power.
PC	Superstar!… What does it mean if you have a lot of will-power, Jon?
Jon	Say if you… had one of those telephone 'phones.
Russell	Telephone 'phones!
Jon	Like those radio 'phones what you carry around.
PC	Oh, yes.
Jon	You'd be making calls just for anything, but you could stop doing it; or when you're smoking, you could give up.
PC	In what sorts of situations do you think we would need to have will-power?…
Matthew H.	Stop eating sweets.
PC	Why would we need will-power to stop eating sweets?… Do we like to eat sweets, Kirsty?
Kirsty	Sometimes.
PC	What's my favourite sweet, Jayne?
Jayne	Toffee?
PC	Well, I like toffee, but it's not my favourite… Caroline?
Caroline	Chocolate?
PC	Bullseye! Chocolate. I like 'Mars' bars. Now, when would I need some will-power, do you think, Samantha, concerning 'Mars' bars?
Samantha G.	Before you eat it.
PC	Why will I need will-power, Tim?
Timothy	Say you've gone on a diet and you couldn't eat one single 'Mars' bar, then you'd need will-power.
PC	Caroline?
Caroline	You could be walking down the street and your friend just walked up to you and said: 'Here, do you want my 'Mars' bar?'
PC	Why would I need will-power there, Caroline?
Caroline	To stop you from saying: 'Yes'.
PC	What other sorts of situations require us to have will-power?
Michelle	Drinking.
PC	Drinking what?
Michelle	Wine, beers and spirits and things like that.
PC	Why do we need will-power when we think about wine and beer? Matthew P.?
Matthew P.	Because you can get addicted to it.
PC	What do we mean by 'addicted'?… Kirsty?
Kirsty	Always wanting some.
PC	Now, say you're addicted to cigarettes…
Russell	My sister.
PC	Your sister's addicted to cigarettes is [she]?
Russell	Not addicted but, not actually addicted, she's tried to stop.
PC	She tries to stop. Does she succeed?

Russell	Sometimes.
PC	Let's say she was never able to stop. Would she be addicted?
Russell	Yes.
PC	Is Knownothing addicted to these sweets?
Russell	Yes.
PC	Melanie?
Melanie	He might not be because he hasn't even tried to stop.
Russell	That means he's addicted then, if he hasn't tried to. He doesn't intend to try, so he's addicted.

| Comment | *According to Melanie, someone is addicted to something only if he or she has tried unsuccessfully to give it up. As Knownothing has not made such an attempt, he might not be addicted. However, Russell argues that since Knownothing has made no attempt to give up sweets, one might justifiably suppose that he does not intend to do so and that, consequently, he is addicted.* |

Richard	Oh, yes.
PC	Any other thoughts? Matthew?
Matthew P.	When I go shooting, and say it's Sunday and I'm shooting for rabbits and a pheasant gets up, I need loads of will-power not to shoot the pheasant.

| Comment | *Matthew provides us with a philosophical 'gold nugget' to be explored: the question of animal rights.3* |

PC	Why do you need lots of will-power there, Matthew?
Matthew P.	So I don't shoot it.
PC	And is your will-power strong enough?
Matthew P.	Yes, most of the time.
PC	But sometimes it isn't strong enough?
Matthew P.	… I haven't shot, I've always missed.
——	Laughter
PC	Is that because you're a bad shot, or is it because you intended to miss?
Matthew P.	Oh, it's because I'm a bad shot.
PC	So, on those occasions when you fired at the pheasant… what would you say about your will-power?
Matthew P.	It wasn't very strong.
PC	What do you think about that question of shooting pheasants…? Is that something that we should all be doing, do you think…?
Russell	No.
PC	Who says: 'Yes'?
——	No one raises a hand.

PC	Who thinks it's something we shouldn't do?
——	Fifteen children raise their hands. Richard does not put his hand up.
PC	Does this mean, Richard, that you think shooting pheasants is a good thing?
Richard	… if you like chicken, you could shoot one and then you might like it, so you carry on.
PC	So, you think it's quite a good thing… to do?
Richard	Yes and no.
PC	Why 'no' then?…
Richard	Because if it's out of the season, you're shooting them, you're not allowed.
PC	So, does that mean when it's out of season, it's a bad thing to do?
Richard	Yes.
PC	But when it's not out of season, it's a good thing to do?
Richard	Yes, because you can go and farmers…
PC	What about farmers?
Richard	They sometimes shoot them.

Comment   *Richard equates what is morally right/wrong with what is lawful/unlawful.[4]*

PC	What do you think about farmers shooting pheasants… Melanie?
Melanie	I think whoever shoots pheasants are cruel.
PC	Why is it cruel?
Melanie	Because, well how would Richard, or whoever shoots pheasants, like a pheasant, or somebody, to come up and shoot him?
——	Laughter

Comment   *Melanie alludes to what might be called 'the universal aspect of ethics' (Singer 1979, p. 11). For example, the 'Golden Rule' enjoins us to treat others as we would have them treat us. The first formulation of Kant's categorical imperative is: 'Act only on that maxim through which you can at the same time will that it should become a universal law' (Paton 1969, p. 84). In suggesting that the purview of our universalizing should extend to non-human animals, Melanie shows herself not to be a supporter of contractual theories of ethics (Singer 1979, pp. 68–71).*

PC	But the pheasants can't shoot us can they, Melanie?
Melanie	No, or whatever – a giant came and shot him. I mean, you know Richard, he's bigger than a pheasant, so… to the pheasant he's a giant.
PC	What's wrong [with] shooting pheasants then… Sally?
Sally	It's cruel and you shouldn't shoot anything because they have a life the same as us.

PC	Why do farmers shoot pheasants then? Russell?
Richard	To get food.
Russell	Because if a pheasant went... in a farmer's field and ate all the crops, they'd have a good right to kill the pheasant.
PC	Why would they have a right to kill the pheasant...?
Russell	Because it ate all the crops.
PC	Let's say you went to the farmer's field and there were some... potatoes there and you thought: 'Yes, I'm going to have some potatoes for my tea tonight. I'll have some'. The farmer comes along... and takes out his shotgun and shoots you, Russell. Is he entitled to shoot you?
Russell	No.
PC	Why is he not entitled to shoot you but he's entitled to shoot the pheasant...?
Russell	Because it's a law not to kill. Like, say if he came up to me and shot me, he'd probably be put in prison. But if he came up to a bird and shot the bird, he wouldn't.
PC	But you said to me, the reason why the farmer is entitled to shoot the bird is because the bird ate his crops. Now, I'm saying to you, if you came along and took some of the farmer's crops, wouldn't he be entitled to shoot you?
Russell	No.
PC	Why not?
Russell	Because we're... he needs a law to shoot us.
PC	O.K. Jon?
Jon	Well, it's illegal to shoot people but it's legal to shoot a pheasant.
PC	The only reason I asked Russell that was because... he didn't say to me the farmer could shoot the bird because it's legal. He said... the farmer could shoot the bird because the bird took the farmer's crops.
Russell	Yes.
PC	So, I'm giving him another example where someone takes the farmer's crops.
Russell	Yes, but the farmer... probably wouldn't shoot us because he'd know he would get ten years hard labour or something like that.
PC	If the pheasant... swoops down on the farmer's field and makes off with a potato... is the pheasant... stealing?
Chorus	Yes.
PC	Matthew P., why is the bird stealing?
Matthew P.	Because the farmer's grew it and done everything to it, and the pheasant just comes and takes it.
PC	O.K. Is the bird stealing, Matthew Hayton?
Matthew H.	No.
PC	Why not?

Matthew H.	Because [the farmer] doesn't know that it's the pheasant… It could be someone coming in the village.
PC	Let's say the pheasant actually takes the potato. Does this mean that the pheasant has stolen the potato?…
Russell	Yes.
PC	Trudelle?
Trudelle	No, because it's what it's supposed to eat. A pheasant can't read… so if there's a sign or something up with the growing potatoes, he can't read that.
Russell	You don't know whether a pheasant can read.
Richard	They're allowed to read a cartridge!
——	Laughter
PC	They can read a cartridge.
Richard	If it hit them!
——	Laughter
PC	Trudelle says the pheasant can't read. Why would that mean, for you, Trudelle, that the pheasant isn't stealing the potato?
Trudelle	Because it's what he's used to eating. It doesn't know that you're not supposed to…
Russell	We're used to eating.
Trudelle	He's used to eating things like that.
PC	When we were discussing the example of the lady who takes the loaf of bread from the shelf in the supermarket… we were discussing all sorts of reasons as to why we might be able to say: 'This person is stealing or has stolen the loaf of bread.' For us to be able to say we had enough proof that she stole it, we needed to prove something about what we called her state of mind. We needed to prove that she _____ to steal it… What's the word I'm after?
Caroline	Intended.
PC	Superstar! We needed to prove that the lady intended to steal the loaf for us to be able to say that, in fact, she stole it, or she was engaged in stealing it. Now, if we could prove that the bird intended to steal the potato – the bird… swoops on to the potato… up and away. That bird has intended to steal the… potato, hasn't it?
Richard	While it's flying, it'll get shot.
PC	What do you think, Jon, has the bird intended…
Jon	It's their way of life. How do they know that you're not allowed to pinch potatoes…? They just think that they're there to eat.
PC	O.K. What if there was an adult who couldn't read? … And let's say the sign in the farmer's field said this:
——	I write 'No Stealing' on the board.
PC	What does the sign say, Michelle?
Michelle	'No Stealing'.

PC	Now, let's say this adult, who comes along to the farmer's field, sees this sign. And this person isn't a very good reader, Caroline, and he thinks it says: 'No Sunbathing'.
—	Laughter
PC	And I say to myself: 'I am starving and there are some potatoes.'
—	I take some conkers from a nearby box.
PC	'Now, what did that sign say again? "No Sunbathing". Yes, I must be all right. [I'll] take these potatoes.' Does this mean the adult hasn't stolen these potatoes?
—	Some children say: 'Yes'.
Richard	He's stolen them.
Russell	He has stolen them!
PC	Russell?
Russell	He has stole them because he still knows that people aren't allowed to steal from farmers.
Matthew P.	He didn't use his common sense.
PC	Matthew?
Matthew P.	He should use his common sense because all people know not to steal from fields or anything.
PC	Now, let's go back to this question of shooting birds... Let's say we see a pheasant in a field and we have our shotgun with us... and we aim at the pheasant. Is that justifiable... Tim?
Timothy	No, because you should preserve wildlife, not destroy it.
PC	Why should you preserve wildlife?
Timothy	Well, because people are always moaning about there's hardly any trees and there's hardly any birds... around, but they're always shooting them.
Russell	Yes, it's their fault.
PC	Why do we need to preserve wildlife, do you think? Aren't these animals just put there for us to eat? After all... do we all have a Christmas dinner?
Chorus	Yes.
PC	What do we have for our Christmas dinner?
Matthew P.	Duck.
PC	What do you have, Caroline?
Caroline	Chicken or turkey.
Russell	Chicken.
Sally	Pheasant.
PC	Who has chicken? Yes, you two... I have a chicken.
Comment	*At this point, it is important not to let it be thought that I am opposed to the idea of eating animals, since this is likely to inhibit children's responses.*

PC	Why do we eat turkey and chicken and duck, do you think?
Richard	Because that's your main meal on Christmas.
PC	Do we ever eat chicken at any other time of the year?
Chorus	Yes.
PC	Why do we eat it?
Matthew P.	Because it tastes nice.
PC	But… you've all been telling me: 'I don't think it's right to shoot a pheasant.'
Timothy	Yes, but there's hundreds of chickens in the world; there's not that many pheasants.
PC	Oh, that's the reason why we don't shoot the pheasant, is it?
Timothy	Because they've got loads of chickens in captivity and they keep breeding them and breeding them, so there's hundreds and thousands of chickens.
Russell	There's hardly ever any pheasants.
PC	So, if there were a lot more pheasants, would that mean that it would be justifiable to shoot the pheasant?
Richard	Yes.
Timothy	Not if they were wild.
PC	Why not?
Timothy	Because it's like, say you were Tarzan and someone came up and shot you. You're wild, so, it's not really justifiable to shoot you.
PC	Well, wasn't there a time when the chickens were wild…?
Russell	Not all of them.
PC	Russell?
Russell	You might have got some in captivity and then them bred. And them ones what they bred… them wouldn't have been in the wild.
Matthew P.	But pheasants are bred in pheasant farms. Last weekend we went to a pheasant farm in Welton.
Richard	There's millions of pheasants.
Chorus	Not as many as chickens.
PC	So, you're saying to me Tim, that if a bird is in captivity, it might be all right to kill it and have it for your dinner. But if it's in the wild, then it's not right to kill it. Is that what you're saying?
Timothy	Yes.
PC	What do we think about that, Sally?
Sally	If, at Christmas, you eat a pheasant or a turkey, you might not have shot it – someone else might have, and you might have bought it.
PC	Now, what's the difference?
Jon	A lot.
PC	What's the difference, Jon?
Jon	You haven't gone out and shot it, so it's not your problem.
PC	Is it not?

Jon	It's there for you to eat; it's shot now and you can't do anything about that.
Comment	*Jon wishes to argue that in instances where one might ascribe moral blame for the killing of an animal, such an ascription should be directed to the killer alone and not to the consumer.*
PC	Imagine the situation in the supermarket, where there are fridges full of chickens... Why do you think these chickens are lying there in the supermarket?
Richard	They've been strangled, not been shot.
Russell	Because they're dead!
PC	Why are they there? What's the purpose of them lying in the shop, Caroline?
Caroline	For us to eat them.
PC	Let us say we all decided today: 'Well, I don't think it's really right to strangle chickens'... Would there be a lot of chickens in the shops in the next few weeks, if everyone in [this village] decided that they weren't going to eat chickens any more, because they didn't like the way chickens are strangled?
Matthew P.	Other people... not from [this village], would go and get them.
PC	Let's say the whole of North Humberside decided that they weren't going to eat chickens any more...
Melanie	But... people might come for a holiday.
PC	But, if a lot of people decided that they weren't going to buy the chickens, would there be much point in killing them and bringing them to the shops?
Russell	No.
Matthew P.	Yes.
Melanie	No.
Richard	If you let them wild and then people might say: 'There's a good bird, I'll shoot it,' and then they'll shoot it, start eating it and then they'll buy it from the shop.
Matthew P.	But, even if we never ate them, they would still be in the shops, because they'll just keep them until you did want them...
PC	What do you think of this argument, Tim, because you said to me: 'It's not really our problem – we didn't shoot the chicken'? What do you say to this: the person who shoots the chicken... or strangles it, is shooting or strangling the chicken because he wants to sell it to a store, to a supermarket, [which] wants to sell it to us...? Let's say we decided we weren't going to eat chicken any more because... we didn't agree with chickens being killed for us to eat. Would there be much point in going around strangling chickens, or shooting them?
Timothy	No.

PC	If you say to me: 'It's not my problem – someone else has shot the chicken or strangled it,' [someone] might say to you: 'Well, if you weren't so intent on having chicken for your Christmas dinner or your Sunday lunch, then these people would never bother shooting chickens or strangling them, and so chickens would just be allowed to live.' What do you say to that argument?...
Timothy	It's a good argument.
PC	Why is it a good argument?
Timothy	Well, because there's nothing really that I can answer back.
PC	Is there something you can answer back, Richard?
Richard	It would spoil Christmas dinner.
PC	Why would it spoil Christmas dinner?
Richard	Because you won't have a chicken or something like that.
PC	What do you think about that, Jon?
Jon	Rubbish!
PC	Why is it rubbish?
Jon	There's thousands of more things what you could have without meat.
PC	Like what?
Jon	You could have real fancy salads and things.
Russell	Yes.
PC	Let's now go back to this question of when we need a lot of will-power. Have we ever been in a situation where we said to ourselves: 'I know that I shouldn't do this...' and then later we say to ourselves: 'Well, I did it after all'... [Has] anyone ever been in a situation like that, where you thought something wasn't the right thing to do, but you did it anyway? Matthew P.?
Matthew P.	I have two [grandmothers]. One lives in Hull and one lives here. And my [grandmother] who was here was ill, so I really should have gone to my [grandmother's] in Hull... I thought: 'I'll go to my [grandmother's] in Hull,' but I never [did].
PC	Where did you go?
Matthew P.	My [grandmother's] here.
PC	Why do you think you did that?
Matthew P.	Just because I could play with all my friends here.
PC	Who was it who... gave me an excellent definition a while ago, who said: 'My head is telling me to do one thing...' Was that you, Michelle?
—	Michelle nods her head.
PC	Would you say that again? 'My head is telling me to do one thing and...'
Michelle	'...the rest of me is telling me to do another thing.'
PC	Now what was happening to your body, Matthew, at the time of this problem you had? Was your head telling you one thing?

Matthew P.	Yes.
PC	What was your head telling you – your brain?
Matthew P.	Not to do it, but my body was getting ready to do it.
PC	Matthew's head was telling him he should go and stay with one grandmother but his body was packing his bag…
——	Laughter
PC	… to go and stay with his other grandmother. Now, do you think the reason for that is that your body was stronger than your brain?
Matthew P.	Yes.
PC	Has anyone ever been in a situation where they've needed some will-power and their brain was telling them one thing and their body was telling them something else, and they decided to do what their head was telling them?… Russell?
Russell	My garage roof isn't that high but… I was going to try and jump off it… but I thought: 'No'.
PC	Why did you think: 'No'?
Russell	Because I could have broke my neck!
PC	So you decided not to do it?
Russell	Yes.
PC	So what your… brain was telling you was stronger than what your body was telling you?
Russell	Yes.
PC	Why do you think sometimes people feel that they should not do something… but they go ahead and do it anyway?
Matthew P.	Because, though deep down they want to do it… the body doesn't want to do it.
PC	Oh, I thought you were telling me it was the body that wanted to do it but the brain didn't.
Matthew P.	It depends what it is.
PC	So, you can change these around can you?
Matthew P.	Yes.
PC	Sometimes it's the brain telling you to do it, sometimes it's the body… Well, if you really wanted to do something, why do you tell yourself to stop? Why don't you just go ahead and do it? Jon?
Jon	Well, in food matters, your eyes are too big for your belly!
PC	What do you mean by that?
Jon	There'll be a big trifle and you go: 'I'll have a bit of that,' and you don't eat it all.
PC	Do you sometimes think to yourself: 'Well, there's an enormous trifle on the table. I should really only have one portion'? But what happens, Jon?
Richard	It's all gone.
PC	Why is it all gone?
Richard	Because you ate it all.

PC	Why did you eat it all?…
Caroline	Because you didn't have any will-power.
PC	Now, are there any other situations that you can think of… where it would be important to have some will-power?… Melanie?
Melanie	Sally's sister and I go to gymnastics and it was our first time on the big bag, because we'd only been going on the little one.
PC	Yes.
Melanie	My head was telling me, I was scared to do it and don't do it, and in the end I did it. It wasn't so bad after all.
PC	So, are there times when it's right to ignore what the brain is telling us?
——	Three children answer: 'Yes' and one answers: 'No'.
PC	Let me ask you another question… in the story, Knownothing says: 'What's the use of trying, if I know that I'm not going to succeed? I may as well enjoy the sweets and save my energy.' What do we think about that?
Timothy	He's got no proof or evidence that he's not going to succeed.
PC	What would count as proof and evidence for us there, Tim?
Timothy	If he throws all his sweets away.
PC	What else might he have done with the sweets, if he wasn't going to give them away?
Timothy	Give them to his friends.
Richard	Put them in his socks!
PC	What use would they have been to him in his socks?
Richard	If he wanted them, he wouldn't like to eat them because they'd be all smelly!
——	Laughter
PC	Sally?
Sally	When [Knownothing] said he was going to eat the sweets and when he did, then he said: 'I wish I didn't do that now.' His friends said… why didn't he put them in their mouths?
PC	Yes. What do you think about that?
Sally	They would have done the same.
PC	So, what do you think about them telling him off?
Sally	Not very good.
PC	Why not, Sally?…
Sally	Because they'd have done the same.
PC	Melanie?
Melanie	It's the same as biting your finger nails though. Why doesn't he put vinegar on them? Put vinegar on them to stop biting your nails – you can put vinegar on the sweets to stop him eating them.
Chorus	Ugh!
Jayne	I like vinegar!
PC	Caroline?

Caroline	What if you like vinegar though?
Russell	Vinegar on sweets!
PC	If you haven't got any vinegar, Caroline, you're going to need a lot more what?
Russell	Salt and pepper!
——	Laughter
PC	Caroline?
Caroline	Will-power.
PC	That's when you're going to need even more will-power. Now, one last question on this story. Knownothing says this to Knowless, when the sun comes out from behind the cloud: 'It seems as though the sun has forgiven you, Knowless.' What do you think about that?…
Richard	No, because the sun can't hear you or see you.
PC	If you think that the sun can't hear you or see you, isn't it possible that the sun might be able to forgive you, Richard?
Richard	No.
PC	Why not?
Richard	Because it can't hear you or see you.
PC	Kirsty?
Kirsty	Just because it's come out again after going in, it doesn't mean to say it's forgiving. It could just have gone behind a cloud and come out.
PC	Yes it might. What would be the word we would use for that, Matthew, that you mentioned before? If a person said something and the sun went behind the cloud, you said that was an example of what?
Matthew P.	Luck.
PC	There's a longer word, as well, that that might be an example of. Can anyone think? Let me see how many letters there are in it. Eleven letters… It would be an example of something beginning with…
Matthew P.	Solution.
PC	We'll have another game of 'Hangman' then.
——	I write eleven dashes on the board: - - - - - - - - - - -
PC	I'll give you the first letter: 'C'. Someone tell me without me giving any more letters. Caroline?
Caroline	Curiosity?
PC	No, it wouldn't be an example of a curiosity… Kirsty?
Kirsty	Coincidence?
PC	Excellent… can you spell it for me Kirsty, please?
——	Kirsty shakes her head.
PC	Well, you don't know until you've tried. You're like Knownothing.
Matthew P.	You have no proof or evidence you can't do it.

Comment	*This is an excellent example of how insights gained in a philosophical discussion can be applied in practical and non- contrived situations in the classroom. Hopefully, such discussions will also be of benefit to pupils in their lives outside school, as insights gained are applied to a broad range of contexts in which children are called upon to think, reason and argue in a critical manner.*
PC	What does she have no proof or evidence of, Matthew?
Matthew P.	She can't do it.
PC	That she can't spell it. Excellent.
——	Kirsty spells the word with some help from one of her class-mates.
PC	Excellent. Not only a class of excellent thinkers but a class of superb spellers as well! Now, I've got something to say to you. That is the best discussion I have ever had with a group of children… Now, what do we think about these people – you remember I mentioned a famous person – what was the famous person's name, Jon?
Jon	Plato.
PC	Why did I mention Plato to you, Jon?
Jon	He said that you can't study philosophy if you're under thirty.
Comment	*In the* Republic, *Plato (1974, Book 7, 537d) argues that dialectic (philosophy) can only be introduced to those who have successfully completed many years of training and study and who have reached the age of thirty (see Chapter 3).*
PC	What do we think about that, Caroline?
Caroline	It's not true because we… you can and he's not including you either.
PC	Jayne?
Jayne	You've got no proof or evidence that you can't do philosophy if you're under thirty.
PC	If I wanted to go and talk to some adults and to say to them: 'I have a group of children… who are capable of engaging in philosophy and they're [eight- to eleven-year-olds]', what would my tape provide for me, Melanie?
Melanie	Proof and evidence.
PC	So, what do we think of Plato's argument, Kirsty, that you can't study philosophy until you're thirty?
Kirsty	Wrong.
Matthew P.	He has not got no proof or evidence.
PC	He has no proof or evidence… This tape, in fact, provides evidence of the opposite… Thank you very much.

Notes

1. According to Mackie (1995, pp. 707–8): *post hoc, ergo propter hoc* ('After this, therefore because of this') is, 'strictly, the fallacy of inferring that one event is caused by another merely because it comes after it. More loosely, the fallacy (characteristic of superstitious beliefs) of assuming too readily that an event that follows another is caused by it without considering factors such as counter-evidence or the possibility of a common cause.' See also Matthews (1985, p. 1).
2. On *akrasia* (incontinence), see Mortimore (1971); Aristotle (1976, Book 7); Matthews (1979, p. 4); Gosling (1995, pp. 19–20).
3. See, for example, Singer (1979, 1986, pp. 215–28); Bowen and Costello (1997b); Almond (1998, pp. 219–22).
4. For a discussion of levels of moral reasoning, see Kohlberg (1984, pp. 170–205); Modgil and Modgil (1986); Rowe (1996); Haydon (1997); Almond (1998).

Appendix 3 – Classroom Dialogue 2

The following dialogue, which took place with Class B1 (children aged six to seven years), focuses on the theme 'Helping others and being helped by others'.

Section 1: Helping other people

MB	The story we are going to hear about Ernie and Bert today is all about helping people – helping people with a problem. Now, have you ever helped anybody that's got a problem?
Robert	Yes.
MB	Robert, when did you help somebody with a problem?
Robert	I help my little brothers when they get hurt.
MB	Do you? And what do you do when they get hurt?
Robert	If they fall over, I just pick them up.
MB	Do you? And try to make them better?
	Robert nods.
MB	Zoe, have you met somebody with a problem and helped them?
Zoe	When my friend fell over, Amy, she cut her leg open and I took her to her mum.
MB	Did you? And she made it better? Ryan?
Ryan	I saw Robert before – and he fell over and cut his knee and I had to help him up.
MB	Anybody helped somebody that didn't fall over, helped someone in another way? Gareth?
Gareth	I helped someone when they couldn't ride their bike.
MB	Did you help to teach them how to ride a bike? Well, that was a nice way of helping someone solve a problem, wasn't it? Amy?
Amy	If I find someone who is sick… I could get them and tell their mum.
MB	Yes, if you find someone who has been a bit sick and poorly. Nicole?
Nicole	If my sister falls over… If my brother needs to ride his bike, I push him on it.
MB	Do you?
Nicole	And start him going.

MB	Good. What about Luke, would you like to tell me…
Luke	I help my big brother and my little brother.
MB	Do you? To do what?
Luke	Because I help my little brother how to learn to ride his bike, because he hasn't got no gears…
MB	Good… Ryan, do you help anybody?
Ryan	My baby brother can't walk up the stairs, so I have to hold his hand and walk up with him.
MB	That's a nice way of helping somebody who's got a problem, isn't it?
Kirsty	When Adam fell over, right, I gave him a biscuit.
MB	Did you, to make him feel better? Is Adam your brother?
Kirsty	And a drink.
——	He always falls over.
MB	That's very good. And Rebecca?
Rebecca	When my sister fell over on glass and she cut her leg open, I had to help my mum when she went to the doctor's and she… (inaudible)
Nico	My brother… we went on a boat and my brother fell in and he was right by the waterfall and I got him out.
MB	Oh, that's a good way of helping.
Robert	If someone falls over and cuts their knee open, I take them to hospital.

Section 2: Introduction to 'Ernie and Bert at the Cinema'

Amy	He had a look in the book because there was a photo in it.
PC	Now that's a good way to start, isn't it? Let's think about that. The lady who introduces this episode in the video is called Gina; and Gina shows Big Bird a book and says this is Ernestine's favourite book because… because what?
Robert	There's a photo in it.
Nicole	Because there's a photo of his friend in it.
PC	And what are the names of Ernestine's friends?
Chorus	Bert and Ernie.
PC	Now Big Bird says: 'I don't think they'd fit in that book', because Gina had said that Ernie and Bert are in the book.
Robert	When he looked in it, it was a photo.
PC	So do we think that children can actually be in books?
Chorus	Yes.
PC	Do you think that they can fit in books?
Chorus	No!
PC	So what do we mean when we say that Bert and Ernie were in the book?

Luke	Because it's a photograph.
PC	It's a photograph and that's how we get into books isn't it?

Section 3: 'Ernie and Bert at the Cinema'

PC	Now at a certain point in this, Ernie decides he is going to swap seats with Bert.
Nicole	He was pushing him off the seat.
PC	He tried to, didn't he, Nicole? Now what do we think about that?
Robert	Unkind.
PC	Why is it unkind, Robert?
Robert	Because he tried to get him off his seat – like spiteful to him, trying to push him off the seat so he could go like that [Robert moves head and body sideways], because the woman had a big hat on.
PC	Now Nicole has said something important there. He didn't…
Nicole	He didn't ask nicely.
PC	He didn't ask nicely. So if that had been you, Nicole, how would you have asked Bert for some help?
Nicole	'Please could I swap seats with you?'
PC	O.K. That would be a nice way to start wouldn't it? Then Bert pushes Ernie off and Ernie thinks again about this problem he has got, because the problem he has got is … he can't…
Nicole	He can't see.
PC	He can't see, so he tries to solve the problem by sitting on Bert's lap. And what does Bert do?
Nicole	He pushes him off.
PC	He pushes him off. Now, Nicole, if that had been you, instead of trying to sit on this other person's lap, what might you have said?
Nicole	'Please can I sit on your lap?'
PC	To see this film. Now in the end, Bert decides to help Ernie and he gives him some advice.
Nicole	Asking the lady, please can you take your hat off. And so she took it off and put it on the other chair and then the other one couldn't see.
PC	That's very good, Nicole. Now let me ask you this: is it fair do you think…
Chorus	No!
PC	Is it fair that Bert now can't see the film because the hat has been put in front of him?
Class	No!
PC	But what do you say to somebody who says: 'Yes it is fair, because Bert wasn't very good at helping Ernie with Ernie's problem and so therefore it is fair'? Who thinks it's fair?
Glyn	Me.

PC	Why do you think it's fair, Glyn?
Glyn	Because he didn't help Ernie properly.
PC	Is there anybody that thinks it isn't fair... it isn't fair that Bert can't see?... Nicole?
Nicole	I don't think it's fair because the other one was sitting there. I think it's not fair because the other one couldn't see first, then the other one couldn't see.
PC	So what would be a good solution if we wanted both Bert and Ernie to see this film? How could we solve the problem of this lady's hat, so that both Bert and Ernie could see? Natasha?
Natasha	Lie it down on the floor.
PC	O.K., that's what we could do, because when we go to the cinema, we don't put our bags, do we, and our ice creams on the seat next to us or on the seat in front. Where do we put them?
Chorus	On the floor.
PC	Now let's leave the story of Bert and Ernie and think a little bit about helping people.
Gareth	There's another way both of them could see. Put it on to the next person.
PC	Now would that be fair? But what if it stopped that other person seeing something, Gareth?
Gareth	I don't know.
Robert	It wouldn't be fair for him, because he wouldn't be able to see then if the lady put it on to the other side, so then Ernie and Bert...
Gareth	I know, put it on the end of the chairs, the very end and stand it up and then she could stand in front of it.
PC	...Now we are going to... think together about ways in which we can help people when they have got a problem. And I also want us to have a think about ways in which people can help us when we've got a problem. Let's start to think about ways that we can help other people...
MB	When you go home tonight, how might you help someone? I'll tell you what we'll do, we'll go around everybody, so that everyone gets a turn to say how they might help somebody at home tonight. Kirsty?
Comment	*The children take it in turns to hold Ernie and then pass him on to the next speaker.*
Kirsty	I'll help my mum tidy up.
Amy	I'll help my mum to do the pots and wash them.
Natasha	I'll help my mum put the washing out.
Rebecca	I'll put the food in the kitchen and help my mum do the shopping.
Charlene	I'll help her to do the rooms.

Kelly	I'll help my mum with…
Zoe	If my little brother falls over, I'll help him up.
Nicole	I'll help my mum tidy up the living room and upstairs.
Luke	I'll help people who fall over and cut their knee.
Nico	I have to polish my bedroom and tidy up.
Ryan	I'm lazy – I don't help.
MB	Well, how might you change that tonight?
Ryan	Tidy my bedroom.
Robert	Go to sleep for my mum.
Lee	Go to bed.
Gareth	When me and my brothers are having a new bed, I'll help my mum get it out of the van.
Stacey	I'll help my mum tidy up the house.
Sabrina	I'll help my mum do the kitchen and the living room.

Section 4: When do we need help?

MB	… Let's go back to thinking now about helping people… I want you to think about a way in which *you* might need help. Is there anything you need any help with and somebody might help you? So, in school, are there any times when you need help? Kirsty?
Kirsty	When I fall over, I go to the teacher.
Amy	When I fall over, somebody comes and helps me.
Rebecca	I listen to my mum.
Nicole	If I fall over, my cousin will go and tell the teacher.
Gareth	If I fall over, I'd just lie there crying.
MB	So if you were crying, who might come and help you?
Gareth	The teacher.
MB	And perhaps some of your friends would come and help you.
——	I'd help him.
Gareth	My friends would come and tell the teacher to come.
Ryan	I would, I'd tell the teacher if I saw it.
MB	Sabrina, would you like to tell us how somebody might help you today?
Sabrina	When I fall over, someone might go and tell the teacher.
Luke	If I fall over on the bench, someone might help me.
MB	Who do you think might help you?
Luke	Teachers.
Ryan	If somebody hit me, the teacher would help me and Robert would help me.

Appendix 4 – Classroom Dialogue 3

The following dialogue, which took place with Class A (children aged five to six years), involves a discussion of school rules and of the concepts 'same' and 'different'.

MB	Remember at the end of the lesson last week, we talked about all the rules that you have up [on the wall]: 'good sitting', 'good listening', 'good looking', 'good thinking', 'waiting your turn', and there's one right at the bottom. What's that?
Chorus	'Talking about the same thing'.
MB	Those are the rules we are going to be thinking about today, when we are working hard, aren't they? Why do you think we have got the rules?
Kelly	So the teacher doesn't get a headache.
MB	So the teacher doesn't get a headache. Oh! that's a good idea. So if you are all well behaved, the teacher doesn't get a headache and she doesn't get cross. Jade, why do you think that we have got the rules there?
Jade	So she doesn't have to repeat them.
MB	So she doesn't have to repeat them. She doesn't have to keep saying to you: 'Now you listen well, Jade', because you know that that is one of the rules and you must do that. Very good. Amy?
Amy	So you'll remember them.
MB	So you'll remember them. Why do you think you have got the rules there? Why do you think they are important? Matthew?
Matthew	Because the teacher doesn't want us to be naughty.
MB	So you think they're rules that stop you being naughty. Or do you think that they are rules that make the classroom a happier place?
Chorus	A happier place.
MB	Why do you think they make the classroom a happier place? Jessica?
Jessica	Because you can do… your work you don't get shouted at.
MB	So there is not a lot of shouting if you follow the rules, so that makes the classroom a happier place with not a lot of shouting going on. Jodie?

Jodie	Just in case you forget.
MB	Just in case you forget. Why do they make the classroom a happier place? Why is it a good idea to have those rules?
Kelly	Because people wouldn't be naughty then.
MB	No, it's not a very good idea in a class is it if everybody's naughty and everybody has to keep shouting... Let's have a think about each of these rules now and I wonder, as we go through them, if you can tell me what they mean. Some, I think, are quite easy to understand but I would like you to explain some of the last ones to me. So the first one is quite easy – 'good sitting'. What does that mean? Oh! You are all showing me how you do that. Lee, what does 'good sitting' mean?
Lee	Cross your legs and fold your arms.
MB	And sit up straight?... What about 'good listening'?
Nathan	Listening good... listening to what the teacher says.
MB	Anybody else want to add anything to what Nathan had to say?
Leigh	'Good looking' because...
MB	'Good listening' we want now.
Leigh	Talking about what the teacher says.
MB	And listening hard?
Lee nods.	
MB	What about 'good looking?' I think you wanted to tell me about 'good looking', didn't you, Leigh? What does that mean?
Lee	Seeing what the teacher's doing.
MB	Seeing what the teacher's doing. Yes, making sure you watch everything that she does, so that you learn from your teacher. What else might it mean, 'good looking'?
Kelly	See what the people are doing.
MB	Seeing what the other people in your class are doing. Yes, you might learn something by looking at them. Jessica?
Jessica	And then you don't get your work wrong.
MB	You don't get your work wrong, no, if you look carefully. That's good. What about 'good thinking'? What does that mean – 'good thinking' – Kelly?
Kelly	If you don't think, you wouldn't be able to do the work.
MB	Wouldn't you? No, I don't suppose you would. What about Leigh? 'Good thinking'.
Leigh	So you don't do your work wrong and...
MB	Naomi, Do you want to tell me something about 'good thinking'?
Naomi	Thinking about the same things.
MB	You have to keep thinking about the same things. So thinking about what the teacher's been saying – is that what you mean? Jessica?
Jessica	I forgot.

MB	Never mind you might remember later. Anybody else want to tell me about 'good thinking', because I think that there is a lot of thinking going on today?
Lee	Thinking about what you are doing.
MB	Thinking about what you are doing, yes, so that you get everything right. What about this one: 'waiting your turn'? What does that mean? Joshua?
Joshua	Put your hand up.
MB	Put your hand up, yes, so that everybody gets a turn and we don't have everybody shouting out. Michael?
Michael	When someone is talking, you don't interrupt them.
MB	Why don't you interrupt someone when they are talking? Chloe?
Chloe	Because it's rude.
MB	It's very rude and you won't be able to hear what they say if everyone keeps interrupting will we? Kelly?
Kelly	Because it wouldn't be fair on the other person then.
MB	No, it wouldn't if you kept interrupting when they were speaking. And the last one down here: 'talking about the same thing'. What does that one mean? Who haven't we had? Lee?
Lee	You have to talk about the same thing. You're not allowed to talk about not what the teacher's talking about.
MB	I see, so if the teacher's talking about the weather outside, you must all talk about the weather outside. Is that what you mean?
Lee nods.	
MB	Anybody else give me an example about that rule or tell me what it means? Bethan?
Bethan	If she's talking about the books – what you are doing in it – if she says 'Have you got any questions?', you have to talk about the same thing.
MB	Same thing. Give the questions about the book and not questions about anything else – is that right? Is that what you mean? Good girl. And Joshua, did you want to say something about that rule? No, O.K. Now at the end of the last lesson, Mr. Costello asked you to think about which of the rules there you thought to be the most important rule to make this a happy classroom. Oh, you've all got ideas. Shall we go around everybody in turn and see which rules everybody thinks are the most important and why? Nathan, which rule do you think is the most important and why?
Nathan	'Good looking'.
MB	'Good looking' – why do you think that's most important?
Nathan	Because if you don't look, then you won't know what to do.
MB	That's very good, yes. Haydn, which do you think is the best rule?
Haydn	'Good thinking'.
MB	'Good thinking' – and why do you think 'good thinking' is the best one?

Haydn	Because if you don't think about it, you won't know what it is meant to be.
MB	That's right, yes. Lee, which do you think is the most important?
Lee	'Good listening'.
MB	Why is that?
Lee	Because if you didn't listen, then you wouldn't know how to do your work.
MB	That's right, good boy. Jessica, which is your favourite? Which do you think is the most important?
Jessica	'Talking about the same thing'.
MB	Why do you think that's most important?
Jessica	Because if you don't talk about the same thing, then you won't...
Alex	If you don't talk about the same thing, you don't know what to do.
MB	Good girl. What about Jodie? Which is your favourite? Which do you think is the most important rule in this class?
Jodie	Thinking.
MB	The 'thinking' rule – why is that? Chloe?
Chloe	'Waiting your turn'.
MB	'Waiting your turn'. Why do you think that's a good rule?
Chloe	Because if you shout out, it will spoil it.
MB	It will spoil the lesson – it will make it very noisy won't it? Bethan, which do you think is a good rule?
Bethan	'Good looking'.
MB	'Good looking' – why?
Bethan	Because if you don't look, you won't know what to do.
MB	Amy?
Amy	'Good thinking'.
MB	Why do you think 'Good thinking' is an important rule?
Amy	Because if you don't think about it, you won't know what to do.
MB	Mike?
Michael	'Good looking'.
MB	And why do you think that's important?
Michael	Because if you don't look, you won't know what to do.
MB	Matthew?
Matthew	Good thinking or you won't get your sums right.
MB	Lucas?
Lucas	'Good listening'.
MB	'Good listening' you think is important and why is that?
Lucas	Because if you don't listen, you won't know what to do and then you'll just say to the teacher: 'I don't know what to do'.
MB	Alex?
Alex	'Good looking'.
MB	Why do you think that's important?
Alex	Because if you don't look, you could hurt yourself if you bang into something.

MB	Joshua?
Joshua	'Good thinking'.
MB	Why do you think 'good thinking' is important?
Joshua	Because if you're on the yard and you bumped into somebody, they would get hurt.
MB	Naomi?
Naomi	'Good listening'.
MB	'Good listening' – and why do you think that's important?
Naomi	Because if you don't listen, you won't know what to do.
MB	Chloe?
Chloe	'Good listening'.
MB	Why do you think 'good listening' is important?
Chloe	Because if you don't listen, you don't know what to do and you have to go and tell the teacher and the teacher doesn't like it because they have to repeat it all over again.
MB	Jade?
Jade	'Good looking'.
MB	You think 'good looking' is important – why is that?
Jade	Because when you are walking in the classroom, you might push somebody over.
MB	Kelly, which do you think is most important?
Kelly	'Good listening'.
MB	'Good listening' – and why is that?
Kelly	Because if you don't listen and you are doing a quiz, the teacher won't repeat it again.
MB	What do you think is the most important one, Jodie?
Jodie	'Good thinking'.
MB	'Good thinking'. Why is that? Leigh?
Leigh	'Good listening'.
MB	Why do you think that's important, Leigh?
Leigh	Because if you don't listen and you are doing your work, you'll get it all wrong.
MB	Those were wonderful answers. Very, very good. So do you think these are good rules that you've got in your classroom?
Chorus	Yes.
MB	Why do you think they're good rules?
—	Because they're important.
MB	And Kelly?
Kelly	Because they will make the classroom a happy place.
MB	We are going to do something different now. We are going to talk about something completely different. Do you know what 'different' means?
Kelly	Talking about a different thing.
MB	Talking about a different thing. What does that mean, that word 'different'? Jodie?

Jodie	If it's got loads of things than the other things, then it's different.
MB	… That's very good.
PC	This is what I'd like us to do now. I'd like us to have a look at the person sitting next to us. So, for example, Nathan and Haydn look at each other; Lee and Jessica; and then Alex and Jody; Chloe and Bethan; Amy and Michael; Matthew and Lucas; Alex and Joshua; Naomi and Chloe; Jade and Kelly; Leigh and Jody. I want you to look at each other and I want you to…
Kelly	To look at each other and see what's different.
PC	Yes, Kelly, what am I going to ask people to do?
Kelly	See what's different to the other person.
PC	Isn't that excellent that Kelly gave me the question before I had chance to say it myself? I want you to look at each other's faces and think about some things that are the same and some things that are different.

Examples given were:
    We've both got brown eyes.
    He's got glasses and I haven't.
    Our eyes are the same colour.
    Alex has got a necklace and I haven't.
    We've got the same face.
    They're both smiling.
    I've got brown eyes and she's got green eyes.
    We haven't got the same colour eyes.
    We've both got jumpers on.
    Amy's got a badge on her jumper and I haven't.
    I've got an earring and Matthew hasn't.
    We've both got trousers on.
    We've both got brown hair.
    He's got shorts and I have.
    He's got yellow hair and I haven't.
    We've both got blue eyes.
    She's got plaits and I haven't.
    We've both got blond hair.
    Kelly's got a bobble and I haven't. I've got a hair band.
    We've both got the same eyes.
    I've got jelly shoes on and Leigh hasn't.

PC	What we are going to do now is play you a section of a *Sesame Street* tape and it is just going to look at children's faces. There are three rules that I want us to think about when we are looking at the tape.
Alex	I know two of them.
PC	You know two of them, Alex, what are the two that you know?

Alex	'Good looking' and 'good listening'.
PC	Excellent – we want some 'good looking' and we want some 'good listening'. We also want some good thinking.
Michael	And 'good sitting'.
MB	'Good sitting' – yes, very good.

Video excerpt from *Sesame Street: We All Sing Together* (song about 'Faces').

MB	You did some good listening there, I hope, and some good thinking and some good looking. Now I want to know what was the same about the faces that you saw on the video? Jade?
Jade	Some had the same blond hair.
Matthew	Some had black hair.
Amy	Some had brown faces.
MB	Right, now shall we have a think about some of the things that were different? So some had brown faces...
Amy	Some had brown faces, some had white faces.
MB	Some had brown faces and some had white faces. Jessica?
Jessica	Some had plaits in their hair and some didn't.
MB	Some had plaits in their hair and some didn't. Lee?
Lee	Some had the same skin.
MB	Some had the same skin. What do you mean 'the same skin'? What colour skin?
Lee	Some had white skin and someone else had red skin.
MB	Yes that's right. Chloe?
Chloe	Some had curly hair and some didn't.
MB	That's right – some had curly hair and some had straight hair. Naomi?
Naomi	Some had hair bands and some didn't.
MB	Some had hair bands and some didn't. Kelly?
Kelly	Some had different colour eyes.
MB	Some had different colour eyes that's right. Jodie?
Jodie	Some had hair bands and some didn't.
MB	Some had hair bands and some didn't. Anybody else like to tell me what was different about some of the faces? Leigh?
Leigh	Some had spots and some didn't.
MB	Some had spots and some didn't. Do you mean freckles?
Jade	Yes.
MB	Were there more things the same about the faces or were there more things that were different about the faces? Nathan?
Nathan	More things that were different.
MB	There were more things that were different. And why is that, Nathan?
Nathan	Because everybody's has got a different face.
MB	Everybody has got a different face.
Nathan	Some had blond hair, some had black hair.

MB	That's right. So who else thinks that there are more things different than the same in that video? More things different about the faces than the same. Kelly?
Kelly	If they weren't different, you mightn't think that they were your friend and you might have said: 'Excuse me' and you might have thought it was Naomi sitting by you and they might have said: 'It's not Naomi'.
MB	That's right. One more question from me. Do you think it matters that you look different?
Chorus	No.
MB	Mike?
Michael	No.
MB	Why doesn't it matter?
Michael	Just doesn't.
MB	It just doesn't. Jodie, do you think it matters that everybody looks different?
Jodie	No.
MB	Why?
Jodie	Because you haven't got the same.
MB	Because you're not the same and that doesn't matter? Jodie shakes her head.
MB	What about Jade? Are you going to tell us?
Jade	Because we weren't born in the same countries.
MB	That's right – and that doesn't matter? Jade shakes her head.
MB	So tell me some more about why it doesn't matter that we're different. Kelly?
Kelly	Because we're all friends.
MB	Because we're all friends. Good girl. Amy?
Amy	If someone was your friend and they came from a different country, it doesn't matter what you look like.
MB	Why is that? Why doesn't it matter what you look like? Kelly?
Kelly	Because you're still friends.
MB	Because you're still friends. That's right, good girl. Michael?
Michael	If you were playing with someone with a different colour skin, you wouldn't say: 'Go away'.
MB	You wouldn't say 'Go away'.
Michael	Because they've got a different colour skin.
MB	You wouldn't say "Go away" because they would still be the same person. Is that what you mean? Michael nods.
MB	Good boy. Chloe?
Chloe	It doesn't matter if you're older than your friends.
MB	No, it doesn't matter if you're different in that way.

Bethan	I'm her friend and I'm older.
MB	Any other reasons because this is my last question today. Just one more chance for people to say: why doesn't it matter that we are different? Would you all like to have a turn to answer that question?
Chorus	Yes.
MB	Nathan, why do you think it doesn't matter that we're different?
Nathan	Because if you're different, you are still the same.
Haydn	Because if someone is different, you can still be their friend.
Lee	If they're different, you can just say: 'Do you want to play with me?'
MB	That's right, yes. Jessica?
	Jessica does not respond.
MB	I'll tell you what we'll do, we'll bring out my old friend Ernie and if you can't think of anything to say, you can pass Ernie on to the next person… Alex, why do you think it doesn't matter that we're different?
Alex	If somebody's brown and they live in a different country…
MB	They can still be your friend?
Alex	Yes.
Chloe	It doesn't matter if you've got brown eyes and the other person has got green eyes; it doesn't matter, you can still play with them.
Bethan	It doesn't matter if you haven't got green clothes on and the other person has got brown clothes on, you can still play with them.
Amy	If someone's a different colour than you, you can still be their friend and you can still play with them.
Lucas	If you're different, if people aren't the same, then you can still play with them if they're your friend.
Alex	If someone says it matters and the other person says it doesn't, you might have an argument.
Jade	Even though my cousins are old, I still play with them.
MB	Kelly, why doesn't it matter that we're different?
Kelly	Because if someone said to the other person: 'Go away' and we saw them, we'd say: 'Come on, you can come and play with us'.
MB	And why would you do that?
Kelly	Because it wouldn't be fair if someone else didn't have anyone to play with.
Leigh	Because if somebody's different and… they think then that they are in your family but they're not.
Jodie	If someone is different and they're not your friend any more, then you go and get another friend.
Amy	If someone has got different shoes, it doesn't matter you can still play with them.
PC	I would like to ask two more questions before we finish… to do with being the same and being different… If you have blond hair, would you be the same person if you then later had brown hair?

Jade	Yes, you would be the same.
PC	Why would you be the same person?
Jade	Because your hair has just changed to a different colour.
PC	But you would be the same person? What do you say, Kelly?
Kelly	You would because if your mum calls you that name then you wouldn't have another name.
PC	That's a very good answer. The second question is: Would you still be the same person if your skin was a different colour? Amy?
Amy	Yes.
PC	Why would you be the same person, Amy?
Amy	If someone had been in the sun and they got brown and the other person hadn't, it would still be the same person.
PC	It would still be the same person. That's a great answer. Kelly again?
Kelly	It wouldn't matter because if they got sunburnt and they got their skin into a different colour, it wouldn't matter.
PC	It wouldn't matter, they'd still be the same. This is my very last question. Which do you think is the most important: how you look or how you behave? Joshua?
Joshua	How you behave.
PC	Why is how you behave more important, Joshua?
Lee	Because the teacher might shout at you.
PC	Why might the teacher shout at you?
Lee	Because you've been naughty.
PC	O.K. Chloe?
Chloe	Because you're not behaving very well.
PC	You're not behaving very well… Why isn't it more important for me to look good rather than behave well? Let's say I look very good, but I don't behave very well. What do you think about me then?
Chorus	You're naughty.
PC	What if I behave very well?
Lucas	You're very good.
PC	What happens if I behave very well?
Joshua	You're a good man.
PC	And what happens to me if I'm a good man?
——	You won't get sent to prison.
PC	Do I get sent to prison if I'm a good man do you think?
Chorus	No!
PC	What happens to me then if I'm a good man?
——	You won't have to go to prison.
Jade	You can stay at home with your wife.
PC	What happens to us if we are good children?
Chloe	We won't get shouted at.
Jade	If you're being good, your mum might take you to the sweety shop and you might get some sweets.

PC   And the last comment from Kelly.

Kelly   If you're at school and you're doing good work, your teacher might think that was excellent and you might get a star.

Appendix 5 – Organisations Engaged in Teaching Thinking Skills

Further information about the teaching of thinking skills may be obtained from the following organisations.

Teaching thinking skills

Institute for the Advancement of Philosophy for Children (IAPC)
Professor Matthew Lipman,
Director, IAPC,
Montclair State University,
Upper Montclair,
New Jersey 07043,
USA.

International Council for Philosophical Inquiry with Children (ICPIC)
Wendy C. Turgeon,
Secretary, ICPIC,
133 Fourth Street,
St James,
NY 11780,
USA.

Centre for Critical Thinking and Moral Critique
Professor Richard Paul,
Director,
Sonoma State University,
1801 East Cotati Avenue,
Rohnert Park,
California 94928-3609,
USA.

Society for the Advancement of Philosophical Enquiry and Reflection in Education (SAPERE)

Sara Liptai,
Secretary, SAPERE,
7 Cloister Way,
Leamington Spa,
Warwickshire,
CV32 6QE.

Centre for Research in Teaching Thinking (CRITT)

Dr Robert Fisher,
School of Education,
Brunel University,
Twickenham Campus,
300 St Margaret's Road,
Twickenham,
Middlesex,
TW1 1PT.

The Citizenship Foundation

Don Rowe,
Director, Curriculum Resources,
The Citizenship Foundation,
15 St Swithins Lane,
London,
EC4N 8AL.

European Philosophical Inquiry Centre (EPIC)

Dr Catherine McCall,
EPIC,
West Quadrangle,
University of Glasgow,
Glasgow,
G12 8QQ.

Society of Consultant Philosophers (SCP)

John Colbeck,
SCP Membership Secretary and Treasurer,
7 Holland Way,
Hayes,
Kent,
BR2 7DW.

European Association for Mediated Learning and Cognitive Modifiability (EAMC)
Ruth Deutsch,
The Binoh Centre,
Norwood House,
Harmony Way,
Victoria Road,
London,
NW4 2DR.

Issues in Personal, Social and Moral Education
Craig Donnellan,
Independence Educational Publishers,
PO Box 295,
Cambridge,
CB1 3XP.

Bibliography

Abbott, L. and Rodger, R. (eds) (1994) *Quality Education in the Early Years.* Buckingham: Open University Press.

Abel, R. (1976) *Man is the Measure: A Cordial Invitation to the Central Problems of Philosophy.* New York: The Free Press.

Aboud, F. (1988) *Children and Prejudice.* Oxford: Basil Blackwell.

Adler, J. and Mason, M. (1998) 'O come all ye faithful?', *The Times Educational Supplement* 25 December, 14.

Allen, R. T. (1987) '"Because I say so!" Some limitations upon the rationalisation of authority', *Journal of Philosophy of Education* **21**(1), 15–24.

Almond, B. (1998) *Exploring Ethics: A Traveller's Tale.* Oxford: Blackwell.

Andrews, J. N. (1990) 'General thinking skills: are there such things?', *Journal of Philosophy of Education* **24**(1), 71–9.

Andrews, R. (ed.) (1989) *Narrative and Argument.* Milton Keynes: Open University Press.

Andrews, R. (1995) *Teaching and Learning Argument.* London: Cassell.

Andrews, R., Costello, P. J. M., Clarke, S. (1993) *Improving the Quality of Argument, 5–16: Final Report.* Esmée Fairbairn Charitable Trust/University of Hull, Centre for Studies in Rhetoric.

Anning, A. (ed.) (1995) *A National Curriculum for the Early Years.* Buckingham: Open University Press.

Anning, A. (1997) *The First Years at School*, 2nd edn. Buckingham: Open University Press.

Aristotle (1976) *Nicomachean Ethics*, revised edn. Harmondsworth: Penguin Books.

Arnot, M. (1997) 'Gendered citizenry: new feminist perspectives on education and citizenship', *British Educational Research Journal* **23**(3), 275–95.

Association for Education in Citizenship (1936) *Education for Citizenship in Secondary Schools.* London: Oxford University Press/Humphrey Milford.

Athey, C. (1990) *Extending Thought in Young Children: A Parent – Teacher Partnership.* London: Paul Chapman.

Atkinson, E. (1998) 'Partisan research and the pursuit of truth', *Research Intelligence*, BERA Newsletter **66**, 18–19.

Baglin Jones, E. and Jones, N. (eds) (1992) *Education for Citizenship: Ideas and Perspectives for Cross-Curricular Study.* London: Kogan Page.

Ball, S. and Bogatz, G. (1970) *The First Year of Sesame Street: An Evaluation*. Princeton, NJ: Educational Testing Service.

Barbalet, J. M. (1988) *Citizenship*. Milton Keynes: Open University Press.

Barber, M. (1999) 'Time now to think about thinking', *The Times Educational Supplement* 7 May, 21.

Baron, J. B. and Sternberg, R. J. (eds) (1987) *Teaching Thinking Skills: Theory and Practice*. New York: W.H. Freeman.

Barrow, R. (1975) *Moral Philosophy for Education*. London: Allen and Unwin.

Barrow, R (1987) 'Skill talk', *Journal of Philosophy of Education* **21**(2), 187–95.

Barrow, R. and Woods, R. (1988) *An Introduction to Philosophy of Education*, 3rd edn. London: Routledge.

Beehler, R. (1985) 'The schools and indoctrination', *Journal of Philosophy of Education* **19**, 261–72.

Bell, J. (1987) *Doing Your Research Project: A Guide for First-time Researchers in Education and Social Science*. Milton Keynes: Open University Press.

Benson, T. L. (1975) The concept of 'indoctrination': a philosophical study. Ph.D. thesis, The Johns Hopkins University.

Berrill, D. (1990) 'What exposition has to do with argument: argumentative writing of sixteen-year-olds', *English in Education* **24**(1), 77–92.

Bettelheim, B. (1976) *The Uses of Enchantment: The Meaning and Importance of Fairy Tales*. London: Thames and Hudson.

Blenkin, G. M. and Kelly, A. V. (eds) (1997) *Principles into Practice in Early Childhood Education*. London: Paul Chapman.

Bogatz, G. and Ball, S. (1971) *The Second Year of Sesame Street: A Continuing Evaluation*. Princeton, NJ: Educational Testing Service.

Bok, S. (1995) 'Golden rule', in Honderich, T. (ed.) *The Oxford Companion to Philosophy*, 321. Oxford: Oxford University Press.

Bonnett, M. (1994) *Children's Thinking: Promoting Understanding in the Primary School*. London: Cassell.

Bonnett, M.(1995) 'Teaching thinking, and the sanctity of content', *Journal of Philosophy of Education* **29**(3), 295–309.

Booth, D. and Thornley-Hall, C. (eds) (1991a) *The Talk Curriculum*. Ontario: Pembroke Publishers.

Booth, D. and Thornley-Hall, C. (eds) (1991b) *Classroom Talk*. Ontario: Pembroke Publishers.

Bowen, M. and Costello, P. J. M. (1996a) *Deadly Habits?* Vol. 1 of *Issues in Personal, Social and Moral Education*. Cambridge: Independence Educational Publishers.

Bowen, M. and Costello, P. J. M. (1996b) *The Rights of the Child*. Vol. 2 of *Issues in Personal, Social and Moral Education*. Cambridge: Independence Educational Publishers.

Bowen, M. and Costello, P. J. M. (1996c) *Issues in Personal, Social and Moral Education: Teachers' Handbook*. Cambridge: Independence Educational Publishers.

Bowen, M. and Costello, P. J. M. (1997a) *Family Values*. Vol. 3 of *Issues in Personal, Social and Moral Education*. Cambridge: Independence Educational Publishers.

Bowen, M. and Costello, P. J. M. (1997b) *What are Animals' Rights?* Vol. 4 of *Issues in Personal, Social and Moral Education.* Cambridge: Independence Educational Publishers.

Bralee, J. (1999) Whose role is it to educate for citizenship? BA thesis, North East Wales Institute of Higher Education.

Bruce, T. (1997) *Early Childhood Education,* 2nd edn. London: Hodder and Stoughton.

Buchmann, M. (1988) 'Argument and contemplation in teaching', *Oxford Review of Education* **14**(2), 201–14.

Callan, E. (1985) 'McLaughlin on parental rights', *Journal of Philosophy of Education* **19**(1), 111–18.

Cam, P. (1995) *Thinking Together: Philosophical Inquiry for the Classroom.* Sydney: Hale and Iremonger.

Carr, W. (1991) 'Education for citizenship', *British Journal of Educational Studies* **39**(4), 373–85.

Casement, W. R. (1980) Indoctrination and contemporary approaches to moral education. Ph.D. dissertation, Georgetown University.

Cassidy, S. (1999) 'Citizenship heads for secondary schools', *The Times Educational Supplement* 14 May, 6.

ChildLine (1996) *Children and Racism.* London: ChildLine.

Children's Television Workshop/Educational Testing Service (1990) *Sesame Street Research: A Twentieth Anniversary Symposium.* New York: Children's Television Workshop.

Chivers, T. S. (ed.) (1987) *Race and Culture in Education.* Windsor: NFER-Nelson.

Citizenship Foundation (1992) *Primary Citizenship Project.* London: The Citizenship Foundation.

Clarke, S. (1984) 'An area of neglect', *English in Education* **18**(2), 67–72.

Clarke, S. (1994) 'An area of neglect revisited', *Curriculum* **15**(1), 13–20.

Clarke, S. and Sinker, J. (1992) *Arguments.* Cambridge: Cambridge University Press.

Clavell, J. (1982) *The Children's Story.* London: Hodder and Stoughton.

Cohen, B. (1981) *Education and the Individual.* London: Allen and Unwin.

Cohen, B. (1982) *Means and Ends in Education.* London: Allen and Unwin.

Coles, M. J. and Robinson, W. D. (eds) (1989) *Teaching Thinking: A Survey of Programmes in Education.* Bristol: The Bristol Press.

Cooper, D. E. (1973) 'Intentions and indoctrination', *Educational Philosophy and Theory* **5**(1), 43–55.

Costello, P. J. M. (1988a) '*Akrasia* and animal rights: philosophy in the British primary school', *Thinking: The Journal of Philosophy for Children* **8**(1), 19–27.

Costello, P. J. M. (1988b) 'Primary school philosophy: open to discussion?', *Links* **14**(1), 11–14.

Costello, P. J. M. (1989a) 'When reason sleeps: arguments for the introduction of philosophy into primary schools', *Irish Educational Studies* **8**(1), 146–59.

Costello, P. J. M. (1989b) 'Supervising teachers of children's philosophy', in George, N. J. and Protherough, R. (eds) *Supervision in Education, Aspects of Education* **39**, 75-81. Hull: University of Hull Press.

Costello, P. J. M. (1990a) Against unjustifiable indoctrination: philosophy in the primary school. Ph.D. thesis, University of Hull.

Costello, P. J. M. (1990b) 'Education for citizenship and the teaching of World Studies', *World Studies Journal* **7**(3), 25–8.

Costello, P. J. M. (1992) 'Down to business: economic understanding and critical thinking in the primary school', in Hutchings, M. and Wade, W. (eds) *Developing Economic and Industrial Understanding in the Primary School*, 83–98. London: PNL Press.

Costello, P. J. M. (1993a) 'Artificial intelligence, determinism and the nature of courage: primary perspectives on philosophical problems', *Curriculum* **14**(1), 35–47.

Costello, P. J. M. (1993b) 'Developing philosophical thinking in schools', in Abbs, P. (ed.) *Socratic Education, Aspects of Education* **49**, 49–65. Driffield: Studies in Education.

Costello, P. J. M. (1993c) 'Authority, moral education and the National Curriculum', *NaPTEC Review* **3**(1), 36–45.

Costello, P. J. M. (1993d) 'Educating reflective citizens', *Citizenship: The Journal of the Citizenship Foundation* **3**(1), 3–5.

Costello, P. J. M. (1994) 'The teaching and learning of argument', in Bottery, M., Brock, C., Richmond, M. (eds) *Politics and the Curriculum*, Proceedings of the 27th Annual Conference of the British Comparative and International Education Society, 72–86. BCIES.

Costello, P. J. M. (1995a) 'Extending children's voices: argument and the teaching of philosophy', in Costello, P. J. M. and Mitchell, S. (eds) *Competing and Consensual Voices: The Theory and Practice of Argument*, 112–30. Clevedon: Multilingual Matters.

Costello, P. J. M. (1995b) 'Education, citizenship and critical thinking', *Early Child Development and Care* **107**, 105–14.

Costello, P. J. M. (1996a) 'Values and the teaching of philosophical thinking', *Curriculum* **17**(3), 132–43.

Costello, P. J. M. (1996b) 'Learning to philosophise and to argue: a thinking skills programme for children', *Analytic Teaching* **17**(1), 49–54.

Costello, P. J. M. (1996c), 'Does OFSTED recommend the teaching of philosophy in schools?', *If... Then: The Journal of Philosophical Enquiry in Education*, **2**, 5–10.

Costello, P. J. M. (1997) 'The theory and practice of argument in education', in Van Lier, L. and Corson, D. (eds) *Knowledge about Language*, Vol. 6 of *Encyclopedia of Language and Education*, 31–9. Dordrecht: Kluwer Academic Publishers.

Costello, P. J. M. (in press) 'Citizenship education, cultural diversity and the development of thinking skills', in Leicester, M., Modgil, C., Modgil, S. (eds) *Political Education, Citizenship and Cultural Diversity*. London: Falmer Press.

Costello, P. J. M. and Mitchell, S. (1995a) 'Argument: voices, texts and contexts', in Costello, P. J. M. and Mitchell, S. (eds) *Competing and Consensual Voices: The Theory and Practice of Argument*, 1–9. Clevedon: Multilingual Matters.

Costello, P. J. M. and Mitchell, S. (eds) (1995b) *Competing and Consensual Voices: The Theory and Practice of Argument.* Clevedon: Multilingual Matters.

Cox, C. and Scruton, R. (1984) *Peace Studies: A Critical Survey,* London: Institute for European Defence and Strategic Studies.

Cox, T. (ed.) (1996) *The National Curriculum and the Early Years: Challenges and Opportunities.* London: Falmer Press.

Craft, M. (ed.) (1996) *Teacher Education in Plural Societies: An International Review.* London: Falmer Press.

Crawshay-Williams, R. (1986) 'The words "same" and "different"', *Thinking: The Journal of Philosophy for Children* **6**(3), 38–9.

Davies, I. (1994) 'Education for citizenship', *Curriculum* **15**(2), 67–76.

de Bono, E. (1985) *De Bono's Thinking Course.* London: Ariel Books/British Broadcasting Corporation.

de Bono, E. (1993) *Teach Your Child How to Think.* London: Penguin Books.

Deegan, J. G. (1996) *Children's Friendships in Culturally Diverse Classrooms.* London: Falmer Press.

Degenhardt, M. A. B. (1976) 'Indoctrination', in Lloyd, D. I. (ed.), *Philosophy and the Teacher,* 19–30. London: Routledge and Kegan Paul.

Denscombe, M. (1998) *The Good Research Guide for Small-scale Social Research Projects.* Buckingham: Open University Press.

Department for Education and Employment (1997) *Excellence in Schools.* London: DfEE.

Department of Education and Science/Welsh Office (1987) *The National Curriculum 5–16: A Consultation Document.* London: DES/WO.

DeVries, R. and Zan, B. (1994) *Moral Classrooms, Moral Children: Creating a Constructivist Atmosphere in Early Education.* New York: Teachers College Press.

Dillon, J. T. (1994) *Using Discussion in Classrooms.* Buckingham: Open University Press.

Dixon, J. and Stratta, L. (1982) 'Argument: what does it mean to teachers of English?', *English in Education* **16**(1), 41–54.

Edwards, A. (1998) 'A careful review but some lost opportunities', *Research Intelligence,* BERA Newsletter **66**, 15–16.

Edwards, A. and Knight, P. (1994) *Effective Early Years Education: Teaching Young Children.* Buckingham: Open University Press.

Edwards, J. and Fogelman, K. (eds) (1993) *Developing Citizenship in the Curriculum.* London: David Fulton Publishers.

Elliot, J. (1991) *Action Research for Educational Change.* Milton Keynes: Open University Press.

Epstein, D. (1993) *Changing Classroom Cultures: Anti-Racism, Politics and Schools.* Stoke-on-Trent: Trentham Books.

Fisher, J. (1996) *Starting from the Child?* Buckingham: Open University Press.

Fisher, R. (1990) *Teaching Children to Think.* Oxford: Basil Blackwell.

Fisher, R. (1996) *Stories for Thinking.* Oxford: Nash Pollock Publishing.

Fisher, R. (1998) *Teaching Thinking: Philosophical Enquiry in the Classroom.* London: Cassell.

Fisher, S. and Hicks, D. (1985) *World Studies 8–13: A Teacher's Handbook.* Edinburgh: Oliver and Boyd.

Flew, A. (1972a) 'Indoctrination and doctrines', in Snook, I. A. (ed.) *Concepts of Indoctrination: Philosophical Essays*, 67–92. London: Routledge and Kegan Paul.

Flew, A. (1972b) 'Indoctrination and religion', in Snook, I. A. (ed.) *Concepts of Indoctrination: Philosophical Essays*, 106–16. London: Routledge and Kegan Paul.

Fogelman, K. (ed.) (1991) *Citizenship in Schools.* London: David Fulton Publishers.

Fountain, S. (1990) *Learning Together: Global Education 4–7.* Cheltenham: Stanley Thornes.

Fox, R. (1996) *Thinking Matters: Stories to Encourage Thinking Skills.* Devon: Southgate Publishers.

Freedman, A. and Pringle, I. (1984) 'Why students can't write arguments', *English in Education* **18**(2), 73–84.

Gaarder, J. (1995) *Sophie's World.* London: Phoenix House.

Gaine, C. (1995) *Still No Problem Here.* Stoke-on-Trent: Trentham Books.

Garforth, F. W. (1962) *Education and Social Purpose.* London: Oldbourne.

Gatchel, R. H. (1972) 'The evolution of the concept', in Snook, I. A. (ed.) *Concepts of Indoctrination: Philosophical Essays*, 9–16. London: Routledge and Kegan Paul.

Gazzard, A. (1983) 'Philosophy for Children and the Piagetian framework', *Thinking: The Journal of Philosophy for Children* **5**(1), 10–13.

Gazzard, A. (1986) 'A discussion by fourth graders of similar and different relationships', *Thinking: The Journal of Philosophy for Children* **6**(3), 40–5.

Gill, D., Mayor, B., Blair, M. (eds) (1992) *Racism and Education: Structures and Strategies.* London: Sage Publications.

Gillborn, D. (1990) *'Race', Ethnicity and Education: Teaching and Learning in Multi-Ethnic Schools.* London: Unwin Hyman.

Glock, N. C. (1975) 'Indoctrination': some pejorative senses and practical proscriptions. Ed.D. dissertation, Harvard University.

Godwin, D. and Perkins, M. (1998) *Teaching Language and Literacy in the Early Years.* London: David Fulton Publishers.

Gorman, M. (1994) 'Education for citizenship', in Verma, G. K. and Pumfrey, P. D. (eds) *Cross-curricular Contexts, Themes and Dimensions in Primary Schools.* Vol. 4 of *Cultural Diversity and the Curriculum*, 102–15. London: Falmer Press.

Gosling, J. C. B. (1995) *'Akrasia'*, in Honderich, T. (ed.) *The Oxford Companion to Philosophy*, 19–20. Oxford: Oxford University Press.

Gregory, I. M. M. (1973) 'Review of I. A. Snook, *Indoctrination and Education* and I. A. Snook (ed.) *Concepts of Indoctrination: Philosophical Essays'*, Philosophical Books **14**(2), 25–8.

Gregory, I. M. M. and Woods, R. G. (1970) 'Indoctrination' *Proceedings of the Philosophy of Education Society of Great Britain* **4**, 77–105.

Greig, G. (1988) 'Hurd's citizen GCSE set for schools', *Daily Mail* 10 October, 2.

Greig, S., Pike, G., Selby, D. (1987) *Earthrights: Education as if the Planet Really Mattered.* London: The World Wildlife Fund/Kogan Page.

Griffiths, M. (1987) 'The teaching of skills and the skills of teaching: a reply to Robin Barrow', *Journal of Philosophy of Education* **21**(2), 203–14.

Guin, P. (1996) 'Education for global citizenship', *Analytic Teaching* **17**(1), 59–62.

Halsall, R. (ed.) (1998) *Teacher Research and School Improvement: Opening Doors from the Inside.* Buckingham: Open University Press.

Hare, R. M. (1964) 'Adolescents into adults', in Hollins, T. H. B. (ed.) *Aims in Education: The Philosophic Approach*, 47–70. Manchester: Manchester University Press.

Hare, W. (1976) 'The open-minded teacher', *Teaching Politics* **5**(1), 25–32.

Hare, W. (1979) *Open-mindedness and Education.* Montreal: McGill-Queen's University Press.

Harnadek, A. (1989) *Critical Thinking: Book One.* Pacific Grove, CA.: Midwest Publications.

Harris, K. (1995) 'Education for citizenship', in Kohli, W. (ed.) *Critical Conversations in Philosophy of Education*, 217–28. London: Routledge.

Hart, W. A. (1983) 'Against skills', *Thinking: The Journal of Philosophy for Children* **5**(1), 35–44.

Haydon, G. (1997) *Teaching About Values: A New Approach.* London: Cassell.

Haywood, C. (1997) 'Thinking as an educational imperative', *Special Children* **100**, 24–7.

Healy, J.M. (1990) *Endangered Minds.* New York: Touchstone.

Heater, D. (1990) *Citizenship: The Civic Ideal in World History, Politics and Education.* London: Longman.

Heater, D. (1995) 'Education for world citizenship', *Citizenship* **4**(2), 29–32.

Hewer, R. (1999) Developing citizenship education in primary schools. BA thesis, North East Wales Institute of Higher Education.

Hewitt, R. (1996) *Routes of Racism: The Social Basis of Racist Action.* Stoke-on-Trent: Trentham Books.

Hicks, D. (ed.) (1988) *Education for Peace: Issues, Principles and Practice in the Classroom.* London: Routledge.

Hicks, D. (1994) *Educating for the Future: A Practical Classroom Guide.* Godalming: World Wide Fund for Nature.

Hicks, D. and Holden, C. (1995) *Visions of the Future: Why we Need to Teach for Tomorrow.* Stoke-on-Trent: Trentham Books.

Hicks, D. and Steiner, M. (eds) (1989) *Making Global Connections: A World Studies Workbook.* Edinburgh: Oliver and Boyd.

Hicks, D. and Townley, C. (eds) (1982) *Teaching World Studies: An Introduction to Global Perspectives in the Curriculum.* London: Longman.

Higgins, S. and Baumfield, V. (1998) 'A defence of teaching general thinking skills', *Journal of Philosophy of Education* **32**(3), 391–98.

Hillage, J. *et al.* (1998) *Excellence in Research on Schools.* Research Report No. 74. Norwich: Her Majesty's Stationery Office.

Hopkins, D. (1985) *A Teacher's Guide to Classroom Research*. Milton Keynes: Open University Press.

Howe, A. (1992) *Making Talk Work*. London: Hodder and Stoughton.

Huckle, J. (1989) 'Lessons from political education', in Hicks, D. and Steiner, M. (eds) *Making Global Connections: A World Studies Workbook*, 11–19. Edinburgh: Oliver and Boyd.

Hugill, B. and Surkes, S. (1988) 'Rumbold on responsibility', *The Times Educational Supplement* 14 October, 2.

Humphrey, N. (1997) 'Should adults be allowed to indoctrinate children in any way they choose?', *The Times Higher Education Supplement* 28 February, 20.

Jordan, B. (1989) *The Common Good: Citizenship, Morality and Self-interest*. Oxford: Basil Blackwell.

Judd, J. (1990) 'Thatcher has her way over school history', *The Independent on Sunday* 1 April, 4.

Kazepides, T. (1991) 'Religious indoctrination and freedom', in Spiecker, B. and Straughan, R. (eds) *Freedom and Indoctrination in Education: International Perspectives*, 5–15. London: Cassell.

Kerry, T. and Tollitt, J. (1995) *Teaching Infants*. Cheltenham: Stanley Thornes.

Kleinig, J. (1982) *Philosophical Issues in Education*. London: Croom Helm.

Kohlberg, L. (1984) *The Psychology of Moral Development: The Nature and Validity of Moral Stages*. San Francisco: Harper and Row.

Kohli, W. (ed.) (1995) *Critical Conversations in Philosophy of Education*. London: Routledge.

Lawrence, F. (1996) 'My manifesto for the nation', *The Times, Features*, 21 October, 14.

Leahy, M. and Laura, R. S. (1997) 'Religious "doctrines" and the closure of minds', *Journal of Philosophy of Education* **31**(2), 329–43.

Leigh, A. (1997) '"Five years ago we had no desks"', *The Times Educational Supplement* 4 July, 18.

Levine, S. (1983) 'The child-as-philosopher: a critique of the presuppositions of Piagetian theory and an alternative approach to children's cognitive capacities', *Thinking: The Journal of Philosophy for Children* **5**(1), 1–9.

Lipman, M. (1982) 'Why aren't thinking skills being taught?', *Thinking: The Journal of Philosophy for Children* **3**(3–4), 45–6.

Lipman, M. (1987) 'Ethical reasoning and the craft of moral practice', *Journal of Moral Education* **16**(2), 139–47.

Lipman, M. (1988) *Philosophy Goes to School*. Philadelphia: Temple University Press.

Lipman, M. (1991) *Thinking in Education*. Cambridge: Cambridge University Press.

Lipman, M. (1993) *Thinking Children and Education*. Iowa: Kendall/Hunt Publishing Company.

Lipman, M. and Sharp, A. M. (1978) *Growing up with Philosophy*. Philadelphia: Temple University Press.

Lipman, M. and Sharp, A. M. (1979) 'Some educational presuppositions of P4C', *Thinking: The Journal of Philosophy for Children* **1**(2), 47–50.

Lipman, M., Sharp, A. M., Oscanyan, F. S. (1980) *Philosophy in the Classroom*, 2nd edn. Philadelphia: Temple University Press.

Loewen, J. W. (1996) *Lies My Teacher Told Me: Everything Your American History Textbook Got Wrong*. New York: Touchstone.

Lomax, P. (1998) 'Researching the researchers', *Research Intelligence*, BERA Newsletter **66**, 13–15.

Louis, J. (1990) 'Lenin gives way to Freudian analysis', *The Times Educational Supplement* 30 March, A15.

Lynch, J. (1987) *Prejudice Reduction and the Schools*. London: Cassell.

Lynch, J. (1992) *Education for Citizenship in a Multicultural Society*. London: Cassell.

MacAskill, E. and Carvel, J. (1996) 'Moral crusade gathers pace', *The Guardian* 22 October, 1.

McGuiness, J. (1995) 'Personal and social education: pupil behaviour', in Best, R. *et al.* (eds) *Pastoral Care and Personal – Social Education: Entitlement and Provision*, 51–8. London: Cassell.

McGuinness, C. (1999) *From Thinking Skills to Thinking Classrooms: A Review and Evaluation of Approaches for Developing Pupils' Thinking*. Research Report No. 115. Norwich: Her Majesty's Stationery Office.

Mackenzie, J. (1988) 'Authority', *Journal of Philosophy of Education* **22**(1), 57–65.

Mackie, P. (1995), 'Post hoc, ergo propter hoc', in Honderich, T. (ed.) *The Oxford Companion to Philosophy*, 707–8. Oxford: Oxford University Press.

McLaughlin, T. H. (1984) 'Parental rights and the religious upbringing of children', *Journal of Philosophy of Education* **18**(1), 75–83.

McPeck, J. E. (1981) *Critical Thinking and Education*. Oxford: Martin Robertson.

McPeck, J. E. (1990) *Teaching Critical Thinking*. London: Routledge.

Martens, E. (1982) 'Children's philosophy – or: is motivation for doing philosophy a pseudo-problem?', *Thinking: The Journal of Philosophy for Children* **4**(1), 33–6.

Matthews, G. B. (1979) 'Thinking in stories', *Thinking: The Journal of Philosophy for Children* **1**(1), 4.

Matthews, G. B. (1980) *Philosophy and the Young Child*. Cambridge, Mass.: Harvard University Press.

Matthews, G. B. (1984) *Dialogues with Children*. Cambridge, Mass.: Harvard University Press.

Matthews, G. B. (1985) 'Thinking in stories', *Thinking: The Journal of Philosophy for Children* **6**(2), 1.

Maykut, P. and Morehouse, R. (1994) *Beginning Qualitative Research: A Philosophic and Practical Guide*. London: The Falmer Press.

Miller, R. B. (1986) 'How to win over a sceptic', *Thinking: The Journal of Philosophy for Children* **6**(3), 46–8.

Minnis, F., Overell, G., Sutton, A. (1990) *The Transformers*. London: BBC Broadcasting Support Services.

Mitchell, S. (1994) *The Teaching and Learning of Argument in Sixth Forms and Higher Education: Final Report*. Hull: University of Hull, Centre for Studies in Rhetoric.

Modgil, C. and Modgil, S. (1984) 'The development of thinking and reasoning', in Fontana, D. (ed.) *The Education of the Young Child*, 2nd edn., 23–45. Oxford: Blackwell.

Modgil, S. and Modgil, C. (eds) (1986) *Lawrence Kohlberg: Consensus and Controversy.* Lewes: Falmer Press.

Moore, W. (1972) 'Indoctrination and democratic method', in Snook, I. A. (ed.) *Concepts of Indoctrination: Philosophical Essays,* 93–100. London: Routledge and Kegan Paul.

Morgan, N. and Saxton, J. (1991) *Teaching, Questioning and Learning.* London: Routledge.

Mortimore, G. W. (ed.) (1971) *Weakness of Will.* London: Macmillan.

Murphy, P. and Irvine, C. (1988) 'Baker argues for a school values code', *Yorkshire Post* 14 October, 9.

Murris, K. (1992) *Teaching Philosophy with Picture Books.* London: Infonet Publications.

National Curriculum Council (1990) *Education for Citizenship.* Curriculum Guidance 8. York: NCC.

Nutbrown, C. (1994) *Threads of Thinking: Young Children Learning and the Role of Early Education.* London: Paul Chapman.

O'Hear, A. (1981) *Education, Society and Human Nature.* London: Routledge and Kegan Paul.

O'Hear, A. (1988) *Who Teaches the Teachers?* London: The Social Affairs Unit.

O'Hear, A. (1989) 'Teachers can become qualified in practice', *The Guardian* 24 January, 23.

O'Hear, A. (1990) 'Not on the citizens' band wavelength', *The Times Educational Supplement* 16 March, 16.

O'Hear, A. (1995) 'Teaching and indoctrinating', in Honderich, T. (ed.) *The Oxford Companion to Philosophy*, 867. Oxford: Oxford University Press.

O'Leary, P. T. (1979) 'The indoctrinated state of mind', *Philosophy of Education 1979.* Proceedings of the Philosophy of Education Society. Normal: Illinois, 295–303.

O'Leary, P. T. (1982) 'Indoctrination and the indoctrinated state of mind', in Cochrane, D. B. and Schiralli, M. (eds) *Philosophy of Education: Canadian Perspectives*, 71–82. Ontario: Collier Macmillian.

Oléron, P. (1993) *L'Argumentation*, 3rd edn. Paris: Presses Universitaires de France.

Park, J-W. (1997) 'Education for democratic citizenship and the community of inquiry: some implications for educational reform in Korea', *Thinking: The Journal of Philosophy for Children* **13**(3), 2–5.

Passmore, B. (1985) 'Call to outlaw preaching of politics in schools', *The Times Educational Supplement* 31 May, 6.

Paton, H.J. (1969) *The Moral Law.* London: Hutchinson.

Paul, R. (1993) *Critical Thinking: What Every Person Needs to Survive in a Rapidly Changing World*, 3rd edn. (revised). Santa Rosa, CA.: The Foundation for Critical Thinking.

Paul, R., Binker, A. J. A., Charbonneau, M. (1986) *Critical Thinking Handbook: K–3.* Sonoma State University: Centre for Critical Thinking and Moral Critique.

Paul, R. *et al.* (1987) *Critical Thinking Handbook: 4th–6th Grades.* Sonoma State University: Centre for Critical Thinking and Moral Critique.

Perkins, D. N. (1993) 'Creating a culture of thinking', *Educational Leadership* **51**(3), 98–9.

Perkins, D. N. and Salomon, G. (1988) 'Teaching for transfer', *Educational Leadership* **46**(1), 131–41.

Perkins, D. N. and Salomon, G. (1989) 'Are cognitive skills context-bound?', *Educational Researcher* **18**(1), 16–25.

Peters, R. S. (1973) *Authority, Responsibility and Education,* 3rd edn. London: George Allen and Unwin.

Pike, G. and Selby, D. (1988) *Global Teacher, Global Learner.* London: Hodder and Stoughton.

Plato (1974) *Republic,* 2nd edn. (revised). Harmondsworth: Penguin Books.

Prescott, M. (1997) 'Schools to teach good citizenship', *The Sunday Times* 25 May, 1.

Price, J. (1999) The role of purposeful social interaction in promoting citizenship education within the primary school classroom. BA thesis, North East Wales Institute of Higher Education.

Pritchard, M. S. (1985) *Philosophical Adventures with Children.* Lanham: University Press of America.

Pugh, G. (ed.) (1996) *Contemporary Issues in the Early Years: Working Collaboratively for Children,* 2nd edn. London: Paul Chapman.

Qualifications and Curriculum Authority (1998) *Education for Citizenship and the Teaching of Democracy in Schools.* Advisory group final report. London: QCA.

Qualifications and Curriculum Authority (1999) *The Review of the National Curriculum in England: The Secretary of State's Proposals.* London: QCA.

Quinn, V. (1994) 'In defence of critical thinking as a subject: if McPeck is wrong he is wrong', *Journal of Philosophy of Education* **28**(1), 101–11.

Quinn, V. (1997) *Critical Thinking in Young Minds.* London: David Fulton Publishers.

Randle, D. (1989) *Teaching Green: A Parent's Guide to Education for Life on Earth.* London: Green Print.

Raths, L. E. *et al.* (1986) *Teaching for Thinking: Theory, Strategies and Activities for the Classroom.* New York: Teachers College Press.

Rich, V. (1990) 'Uncle Joe toppled by heirs of Genghis Khan', *The Times Higher Educational Supplement* 2 March, 10.

Robson, S. and Smedley, S. (eds) (1996) *Education in Early Childhood: First Things First.* London: David Fulton Publishers.

Rodd, J. (1998) *Leadership in Early Childhood,* 2nd edn. Buckingham: Open University Press.

Roddy, J. (1981) 'Thinking about thinking and talking about thought', *Thinking: The Journal of Philosophy for Children* **3**(1), 4–7.

Rowe, D. (1992) 'The citizen as a moral agent: the development of a continuous and progressive conflict-based citizenship curriculum', *Curriculum* **13**(3), 178–87.

Rowe, D. (1996) 'Developing spiritual, moral and social values through a citizenship programme for primary schools', in Best, R. (ed.) *Education, Spirituality and the Whole Child*, 285–93. London: Cassell.

Rowe, D. (1998) 'The education of good citizens: the role of moral education', *Forum* **40**(1), 15–17.

Rowe, D. and Newton, J. (eds) (1994) *You, Me, Us! Social and Moral Responsibility for Schools*. London: Citizenship Foundation/The Home Office.

Rowley, C. and Toye, N. (1996) 'Learning to listen, beginning to understand: the skills of philosophical inquiry', in Steiner, M. (ed.) *Developing the Global Teacher*, 83–92. Stoke-on-Trent: Trentham Books.

Ruggiero, V. R. (1988) *Teaching Thinking Across the Curriculum*. New York: Harper and Row.

Ryle, G. (1949) *The Concept of Mind*. Harmondsworth: Penguin Books.

Sale, J. (1984) 'Learning how to ask awkward questions', *The Guardian* 28 August, 9.

School Curriculum and Assessment Authority (1995) *Spiritual and Moral Development*. Discussion Paper No. 3. London: SCAA.

Schrag, F. (1988) *Thinking in School and Society*. London: Routledge.

Scruton, R. (1985) *World Studies: Education or Indoctrination?* London: Institute for European Defence and Strategic Studies.

Scruton, R. (1990) 'Why state education is bad for children', *The Sunday Telegraph* 11 February, 21.

Scruton, R. (1997) *Modern Philosophy: An Introduction and Survey*. London: Arrow.

Scruton, R., Ellis-Jones, A., O'Keeffe, D. (1985) *Education and Indoctrination*. Middlesex: Education Research Centre.

Selby, D. (1995) *Earthkind: A Teachers' Handbook on Humane Education*. Stoke-on-Trent: Trentham Books.

Sharma, Y. (1996) 'Concern over forced ignorance', *The Times Educational Supplement* 22 November, 16.

Sharp, A. M. (1984) 'Philosophical teaching as moral education', *Journal of Moral Education* **13**(1), 3–8.

Sharrock, D. and Linton, M. (1988) 'Electronic tags hailed as part of assault on "dependency culture"', *The Guardian* 13 October, 4.

Siegel, H. (1991) 'Indoctrination and education', in Spiecker, B. and Straughan, R. (eds) *Freedom and Indoctrination in Education: International Perspectives*, 30–41. London: Cassell.

Singer, P. (1979) *Practical Ethics*. Cambridge: Cambridge University Press.

Singer, P. (1986) 'All animals are equal', in Singer, P. (ed.) *Applied Ethics*, 215–28. Oxford: Oxford University Press.

Smidt, S. (1998) *A Guide to Early Years Practice*. London: Routledge.

Smith, R. (1987) 'Skills: the middle way', *Journal of Philosophy of Education* **21**(2), 197–201.

Snook, I. A. (1972a) *Indoctrination and Education.* London: Routledge and Kegan Paul.

Snook, I. A. (ed.) (1972b) *Concepts of Indoctrination: Philosophical Essays.* London: Routledge and Kegan Paul.

Spencer, D. (1990) 'Romanian evacuees anxious to go back', *The Times Educational Supplement* 5 January, 1 and 7.

Spiecker, B. (1987) 'Indoctrination, intellectual virtues and rational emotions', *Journal of Philosophy of Education* **21**(2), 261–6.

Spiecker, B. (1991) 'Indoctrination: the suppression of critical dispositions', in Spiecker, B. and Straughan, R. (eds) *Freedom and Indoctrination in Education: International Perspectives*, 16–29. London: Cassell.

Steiner, M. (ed.) (1996) *Developing the Global Teacher.* Stoke-on-Trent: Trentham Books.

Sutcliffe, R. and Williams, S. (1999) 'The murder of Stephen Lawrence', *If...Then: The Journal of Philosophical Enquiry in Education* **6**, 28–40.

Taylor, M., Hill, C., Lines, A. (1998) *Evaluation of the Citizenship Foundation's Primary School Materials, You, Me, Us! Final Report to the Citizenship Foundation.* Slough: National Foundation for Educational Research.

The Times Educational Supplement (1983) 'Warning on propaganda posing as peace studies', 27 July, 8.

The Times Educational Supplement (1985) 'World Studies "propaganda" – Scruton', 13 December, 5.

The Times Educational Supplement (1986) 'Tories declare war on indoctrination', 7 March, 6.

Thiessen, E. J. (1982) 'Indoctrination and doctrines', *Journal of Philosophy of Education* **16**(1), 3–17.

Thomson, A. and O'Leary, J. (1996) 'Carey's moral crusade upsets schools', *The Times* 6 July, 1.

Thompson, K. (1972) *Education and Philosophy: A Practical Approach.* Oxford: Basil Blackwell.

Tomlinson, S. (1992) 'Citizenship and minorities', in Baglin Jones, E. and Jones, N. (eds) *Education for Citizenship: Ideas and Perspectives for Cross-Curricular Study*, 35–50. London: Kogan Page.

Tooley, J. with Darby, D. (1998) *Educational Research: A Critique.* London: Office for Standards in Education.

Troyna, B. (1993) *Racism and Education.* Buckingham: Open University Press.

Turner, J. (1996) 'Laura and Paul do profundity', *The Guardian Weekend* 8 June, 22–8.

Verma, G. K. and Pumfrey, P. D. (eds) (1994) *Cultural Diversity and the Curriculum, Vol. 4, Cross-Curricular Contexts, Themes and Dimensions in Primary Schools.* London: Falmer Press.

Vulliamy, G. (1998) 'A complete misunderstanding of our position... trivialises our arguments', *Research Intelligence*, BERA Newsletter **66**, 17–18.

Wagner, P. A. Jr. (1978) Indoctrination and moral education. Ph.D. dissertation, University of Missouri.

Wagner, P. A. Jr. (1981) 'Moral education, indoctrination and the principle of minimising substantive moral error', *Philosophy of Education 1981.* Proceedings of the Philosophy of Education Society. Normal: Illinois, 191–8.

Walker, R. (1989) *Doing Research: A Handbook for Teachers.* London: Routledge.

Walsh, P. (1993) *Education and Meaning: Philosophy in Practice.* London: Cassell.

Warnock, M. (1988) *A Common Policy for Education.* Oxford: Oxford University Press.

Watts-Miller, W. and Whiteside, S. (1988) 'Art, education and politics: an interview with Roger Scruton', *Cogito* **2**(3), 1–5.

Webb, R. (ed.) (1990) *Practitioner Research in the Primary School.* Basingstoke: Falmer Press.

Weston, A. (1992) *A Rulebook for Arguments.* Indianapolis: Hackett Publishing Company.

Whalley, M. J. (1984) 'The practice of philosophy in the elementary school classroom', *Thinking: The Journal of Philosophy for Children* **5**(3), 40–2.

Whalley, M. J. (1987) 'Unexamined lives: the case for philosophy in schools', *British Journal of Educational Studies* **35**(3), 260–80.

White, J. (1972) 'Indoctrination without doctrines?', in Snook, I. A. (ed.) *Concepts of Indoctrination: Philosophical Essays*, 190–201. London: Routledge and Kegan Paul.

White, J. (1992) 'The roots of philosophy', in Griffiths, A. P. (ed.) *The Impulse to Philosophise*, 73–88. Cambridge: Cambridge University Press.

White, P. (1996) *Civic Virtues and Public Schooling: Educating Citizens for a Democratic Society.* New York: Teachers College Press.

Whitebread, D. (ed.) (1996) *Teaching and Learning in the Early Years.* London: Routledge.

Wiggan, T. (1999) Implementing an education for citizenship programme in the primary classroom. BA thesis, North East Wales Institute of Higher Education.

Wilkinson, A. (1990) 'Argument as a primary act of mind', *English in Education* **24**(1), 10–22.

Wilks, S. E. (1995) *Critical and Creative Thinking: Strategies for Classroom Inquiry.* Armadale: Eleanor Curtain Publishing.

Woditsch, G. A. with Schmittroth, J. (1991) *The Thoughtful Teacher's Guide to Thinking Skills.* Hillsdale, NJ.: Lawrence Erlbaum.

Woods, P. and Jeffrey, B. (1996) *Teachable Moments: The Art of Teaching in Primary Schools.* Buckingham: Open University Press.

Wright, D. (1971) *The Psychology of Moral Behaviour.* Harmondsworth: Penguin Books.

Wright, J. C. and Huston, A. C. (1995) *Effects of Educational TV Viewing of Lower Income Preschoolers on Academic Skills, School Readiness, and School Adjustment One to Three Years Later: A Report to Children's Television Workshop.* University of Kansas: Centre for Research on the Influences of Television on Children.

Wringe, C. (1992) 'The ambiguities of education for active citizenship', *Journal of Philosophy of Education* **26**(1), 29–38.

Young, S. (1996) 'Party leaders leap on Lawrence bandwagon', *The Times Educational Supplement* 25 October, 6.

Index